MURDER & MAYHEM
IN DAYTON
——— AND THE ———
MIAMI VALLEY

SARA KAUSHAL

THE
History
PRESS

Published by The History Press
Charleston, SC
www.historypress.com

First published 2021

ISBN 9781540248305

Library of Congress Control Number:2021934609

This book is dedicated to my dad, who loved true crime and history.

CONTENTS

PREFACE

As a lifelong resident of the Dayton area, I grew up knowing bits and pieces of local history. You can't go to Kettering schools without learning about Charles Kettering, and you certainly can't live in the vicinity of Dayton without learning about the Wright brothers. My interest in Dayton history came from a conversation about our namesake, Jonathan Dayton.

Dayton was a Revolutionary War veteran and the youngest signer of the U.S. Constitution. I found this information fascinating and shared it with anyone who would listen. This inspired me to start my blog, *Dayton Unknown*. Since 2014, *Dayton Unknown* has shared information about the Dayton area, both historical and current. It was through the years researching and writing for this blog that I gathered enough information to write this book.

ACKNOWLEDGEMENTS

There are many people I want to thank for their help in getting me to this point. I couldn't have done this without the help of the librarians in the Dayton Room at the downtown branch of the Dayton Metro Library. I'd like to also thank the Wright Library and the Xenia Community Library for providing lots of information and quiet places to work.

Many thanks to Stephen Grismer from the Dayton Police History Foundation and Andrew Walsh, author of *Lost Dayton*. I got a lot of helpful information from you both. To John Rodrigue of The History Press, I must have asked you about one thousand questions, all of which you answered patiently.

MOST OF ALL, I'D like to thank my friends and family for their endless support and cheerleading during the past year. To my mother, I want to thank you for always being my supporter. You were the first person I told when I knew this was going to happen. Beth (any), you are the other half of *Dayton Unknown* and my best friend. A most special thank you to my husband, Ravi, my biggest fan and my companion on way too many Saturday trips to the library. You know all the stories almost as well as I do.

THE BALLAD OF JOHN McAFEE

John McAfee entered history in a way most people would not desire. While many achieve a name in history from deeds of great historical or political significance, McAfee's name was written into history another way. McAfee achieved infamy by becoming the first person to be hanged in the young city of Dayton, Ohio, in 1825.

John McAfee was raised by his aunt and uncle for most of his childhood. His parents died when he was young. First was his mother, when he was so young that he didn't remember her. His father remarried a few years later, but then he too met a tragic fate. Andrew McAfee drowned in a sinking ship on the Susquehanna River. After this tragedy, McAfee was taken in by his father's sister, Margaret McAfee Skelly, and her husband, Philip Skelly.

It is unclear why McAfee was so restless in life or when exactly it started. Perhaps he always had the restless spirit in him, or maybe it came later, after he lost his parents in devastating blows. Whatever the reason, McAfee desired to seek out new places and meet new people. This wanderlust led him to move from his hometown of Huntington, Pennsylvania, to the recently opened territory, the Northwest, and then ultimately Dayton, Ohio.

After settling into Dayton, McAfee married the daughter of a Dayton pioneer. Their marriage was initially a happy one, but before long, the honeymoon ended. Although a married man, McAfee was not a settled man. He stayed out all night drinking to excess and enjoying the company of fellow partiers and other rowdy locals. As his wild ways escalated, his social standing in the community dropped. Many who thought highly of him had changed their minds when they saw his outrageous behavior. As many lowered their opinion of McAfee, one stood out, noticing him in a positive light—next-door neighbor Hetty Shoup.

Like a siren call, McAfee was drawn to her. Hetty encouraged him, thrilled by his attention. Some even theorized that she went as far as suggesting to McAfee that he could dispose of his wife for them to move their clandestine relationship into the open. Although he balked at the suggestion initially, he eventually succumbed to the pressure.

Mrs. McAfee had taken to her bed in illness in May 1824. For several weeks, she remained in bed, too weak to care for herself and their infant daughter. When her husband brought her an elixir he said would make her feel better, she was all too willing to drink it. Unfortunately for Mrs. McAfee, the elixir was not intended to make her well but instead to poison her. As she lay in her bed next to their infant daughter, she slowly succumbed to the poison. Impatient, McAfee decided she wasn't dying fast enough. To speed things along, he strangled her in the bed they shared, next to the daughter they created. When the deed was done, he experienced instant regret for his actions and even an intense dislike for Hetty Shoup. At the thought of his behavior and Hetty, he recoiled and fled the house.

Hours later, a neighbor of the McAfees came to check on her condition and discovered her lifeless body. Next to her body on the bed was her crying infant daughter. The neighbor ran to Magistrate Heck for help, and immediately, the town started its search for McAfee. The search was not successful though; McAfee was nowhere to be found.

Days later, McAfee resurfaced at his wife's funeral. During the service, as the preacher was giving his sermon, McAfee appeared. Magistrate Heck whispered to the preacher to cut his service short. Once it ended, McAfee was apprehended. With the assistance of two other men attending the services, Heck tied McAfee with the rope they used to lower his dead wife's coffin into the ground.

The grand jury took no time indicting McAfee for murder in the first degree. The criminal trial was speedy as well, with a guilty verdict returned after a very brief deliberation. On the charge of murder in the first degree, the penalty was death by hanging. With the public sentiment so negative and angry toward McAfee, officials decided not to take a long period of time to carry out the sentence. A crude scaffolding was built, and in late March 1825, Dayton's first hanging was carried out. People from all over Dayton attended the hanging, some spectators even traveling overnight from nearby cities to witness the spectacle. Among the crowd of spectators stood Hetty

Shoup, the vixen who had so tempted McAfee just months before. If she felt anything about the scene unfolding before her, her expression did not give it away. To anyone who didn't know the story, she appeared to be just another onlooker in the crowd.

On the scaffold, McAfee stood expressionless to face his death. During his time in jail awaiting his execution he had expressed remorse for his crime, even writing out a poem that was both a confession of his crime and a warning to young men:

> Draw near young man and hear from me
> my sad and mournful history.
> And may you ne'er forgetful be
> of all this day I fell to thee.
>
> Before I reached my fifth year,
> my father and my mother dear
> were both laid in their silent grave
> by Him who their being gave.
>
> No more a mother's love I shared,
> no more a mother's voice I heard,
> no more was I a father's joy—
> I was a helpless orphan boy.
>
> But Providence, the orphan's friend,
> a kind relief did quickly send,
> and snatched from want and perjury
> poor little orphan McAfee.
>
> Beneath my uncle's friendly roof,
> from want and danger far aloof,
> nine years was I most kindly reared
> and oftimes his advice I heard.
>
> But I was thoughtless, young and gay,
> oftimes I broke the Sabbath day.
> In wickedness I took delight,
> and oftimes did what was not right.

When my uncle would chide me,
I'd turn from him dissatisfied
and join again in wickedness,
and Satan serve with eagerness.

At length arrived the fatal day
when from my home I ran away.
And to my sorrowing in life,
I took to me myself a wife.

And she was kind and good to me
as any woman need to be.
And would have been alive no doubt,
had I not met Miss Hetty Shoup.

Full well I mind that very day
when Hetty stole my heart away.
It was love for her controlled my will
and caused me my wife to kill.

It was one pleasant summer night
when all was still; the stars shone bright.
My wife was lying in the bed
When I approached her and said:

"Dear wife, here's a medicine I've brought
which for you this day I brought.
My dear, I know it will cure you
of the wild fits—pray take it, do."

She gave me a tender look,
and in her mouth the poison took,
and down by her babe upon the bed,
to her last long sleep she laid.

But fearing that she was not dead,
my hands upon her throat I laid,
and then such deep impression made
her soul from her body fled.

Then was my head filled full of sorrow,
I cried as whither shall I go.
How shall I leave this mournful place?
The world again how shall I face?

I freely gave up my store,
if I'd a thousand pounds or more,
if I could bring again to life
my dear, my darling, murdered wife.

Her body now beneath the sod,
her soul, I hope, is with her God,
and soon into eternity
my guilty soul shall also be.

Young man, be warned by me—
pray shun all evil company!
Walk in the ways of righteousness
and God your soul will surely bless.

The minute now is drawing nigh
when from this world my soul will fly
to meet Jehovah at His bar
and there my final sentence hear.

Dear friends, I bid you all adieu,
If on earth I no more see you.
On heaven's bright and flowery plane
I hope we all shall meet again.

BUCKET BRIGADE

A t an early point in Dayton history, there existed no paid fire department. In its place, Dayton used a volunteer "Bucket Brigade." Essentially, volunteers stood in line and passed buckets of water hand to hand from one to another down the line from the source of the water to the fire to put it out. In later years, the same volunteers and bucket line were used to fill the hand-pumped engine that sprayed water to douse the fire. This was an early model of the present-day fire truck. Early Dayton employed this technique with a team of volunteer firefighters and fire wardens.

On the morning of September 10, 1833, a fire alarm rang out. Per usual, the entire town lined up to witness the spectacle. One of the city's fire wardens, a man named Charles Greene, was responsible for organizing the response efforts at the scene and organizing the lineup of volunteers in a row to fight the fire. Greene was one of the first fire wardens in Dayton and one of the first members of the board of directors of the Dayton Manufacturing Company and had also been appointed to succeed Benjamin Van Cleve as clerk of the Montgomery County Court of Common Pleas in 1822. In the midst of this madness, Greene noticed one of the volunteers in the bucket brigade was not lined up properly with the other men. Matthew Thompson was standing a considerable distance away from the group. Seeing a man out of line at this urgent time annoyed Greene, and he yelled for Thompson to get in line.

When Thompson refused to get back in line, Greene attempted to use his position of power to compel Thompson into place. The disagreement between the two men escalated quickly. Their altercation culminated with Greene knocking Thompson's hat off using a splinter of wood that had been nearby. This action infuriated Thompson, and after more words were exchanged, Greene struck Thompson on the head with the same splinter of wood.

Thompson swore revenge against Greene but let it go for the day. The next morning, still seeking some sort of retaliation against his newly sworn enemy, Thompson asked around town if anyone knew where Greene was, and he swore he would have justice for the misdeeds that occurred the previous day.

Artist Depiction of the Bucket Brigade in action during a fire. *Dayton Daily News, courtesy of newspapers.com.*

Word spread and reached Greene later that day. He was not worried, however, and brushed off the comments and warnings from the others in town and went about his day as normal. Meanwhile, Thompson was out getting drunk and stewing, getting angrier by the minute. Perhaps from goading by some of his friends or the fellows in the bar, Thompson's anger reached a boiling point, and he decided he needed to take action immediately.

His first stop was to see a magistrate and demand a warrant against Greene for assault and battery. The magistrate put him off, telling him to try to resolve his issue face-to-face with Greene before pursuing legal action. Thompson argued with the magistrate, declaring that he would not rest until he had "put Greene asleep."

Not getting the warrant, Thompson went to another magistrate, who also tried to get him to settle the issue with Greene before legal action was taken. Seeing that Thompson would not be put off, this magistrate said he would only issue the warrant if the fees were first paid in full. As Thompson was determined to get the warrant, he quickly left to procure the money. When he returned, he paid the fee and demanded for the warrant to be issued.

Greene had been notified by others of Thompson's actions as he attempted to seek justice, so he went to the courthouse to confront him. During this encounter, Thompson asked Greene why he struck him during the fire incident, to which Greene replied that not only did he strike him in the line of duty, but also if he had to do it all over again, he would strike him again, perhaps even harder. The snarky comment incited more agitation between the two men as they argued. Witnesses noted that the argument

Artist depiction of Matthew Thompson attacking Charles Greene. Dayton Daily News, *courtesy of newspapers.com.*

appeared to dwindle and settle as both men seemed to lose interest. As the argument fizzled, Greene turned to leave. He did not anticipate what would happen when he turned his back.

The moment Greene turned his back, Thompson picked up a hickory stick he saw lying nearby. Thompson struck Greene as hard as he could on the right side of his head. Whether he struck Greene by impulse or premeditated plan, we will never know.

Greene was swiftly given medical attention, which included attempts at revival and a call for a surgeon. The medical treatment determined that although his skull had not been fractured, he had sustained a severe concussion. Unfortunately for Greene, he experienced the worst-case scenario for concussions, suffering from vomiting and excruciating pain before ultimately succumbing to his injury. An autopsy revealed extensive bleeding of the brain, from which no operation or medical treatment could have saved him.

Businesses closed the day of Greene's funeral, and a large crowd gathered to pay their last respects at Woodland Cemetery. Greene left behind a wife and six children.

After eight months of imprisonment, Thompson's trial for murder began. The case was speedy, lasting only three days from indictment to conviction. Matthew Thompson was convicted of second-degree murder with a recommendation of "penitentiary for life."

3

'TIL DEATH DO US PART

In June 1849, Jesse Ransbottom was arrested in Greene County for stealing a cow. He was fined thirty dollars and sentenced to five days in jail. This was not Jesse's first time in trouble with the law. Officers from Montgomery County had tried to arrest Jesse for other crimes, but Jesse's wife, Fanny, had argued so valiantly for her husband that the officers backed off. During Jesse's five days in jail, he was only allowed bread and water as meals. On his release, a voraciously hungry Jesse learned Fanny and their four children had been assisted with food while he was in jail. When the neighbors in the small village of Fairfield learned of Jesse's upcoming jail sentence and that he would be unable to provide for Fanny and the children, they came together and made sure the family did not starve. Feeling hungry and angry, or *hangry* by modern terms, Jesse was enraged. Why did he have to go hungry in jail while his wife and children ate plenty?

Once he was released, he headed straight for his home to confront his wife. Since the house was empty, he sat down at the kitchen table to wait for Fanny. As soon as she returned home, Fanny took one look at her husband sitting at the table waiting for her and she knew there would be trouble. Jesse had a history of violent behavior, and Fanny knew the moment she saw him that she should run. Without hesitation, she turned and fled. Jesse gave chase, quickly catching up to her, and as soon as he did, they struggled briefly until she fell, her throat cut from ear to ear by the razorblade he held in his hand.

Neighbors were drawn to the sound of Fanny's screams and calls for help. As they reached her, they realized in horror that they were too late to help—there was nothing they could do for her. Not only had he cut her throat, but he had also stabbed Fanny twice in the chest. Jesse left her body on the ground at the spot where he caught up to her, just a short distance from their home.

He fled from the neighbors, threatening to stab anyone who attempted to apprehend him. In his home, Jesse attempted to cut his own throat but managed to make only a few shallow cuts that did not draw blood. Instead, he decided to wait for the hangman's noose, he later said. Having given up on the suicide effort, he made no attempt to escape or resist when he was arrested.

When asked why he didn't go through with cutting his own throat, he simply replied, "It hurt too much."

Instead of taking his own life, Jesse originally thought it would be better to let the hangman do his job. After being in jail for a bit, he changed his mind. Not only did Jesse now want to live, but he also did not want to pay for his crime. Jesse started giving excuses for why he could not be held responsible for his conduct. Jesse claimed that when he worked in the coal mines, he was injured and, as a result, was unable to control his actions.

Prosecution was Joseph G. Gest, assisted by a man named Gatch. Ellsberry and Sexton represented the defense, and Judge Vance presided over the case. Jesse's attorneys tried to delay the trial for various reasons, including an attempt to get testimony from Pennsylvania and the unexpected death of Jesse's brother, Walker Ransbottom, before the trial began. Walker had been en route to Xenia to be at Jesse's trial but was found dead in Springboro on October 16, two days before the trial. He had been staying in a room above Hall's Eating House. The company he kept the night before reported that he had not complained of any illness or injury. The coroner ruled Walker Ransbottom's death a result of apoplexy.

These attempts to delay the trial were overruled not only by the court but also by none other than Jesse Ransbottom himself, as he didn't want to be kept in suspense about his fate any longer than necessary.

Jurors for the trial were Bennett Lewis, Peter Babb, Walter Parry, Nathan Plowman, William Baker, Michael Dougherty, George Glotfelter, James A. Brown, Samuel McCoy, Abraham Ellis, John D. Burrill and David Puterbaugh.

When the trial began on October 18, 1849, twenty-five witnesses presented evidence to the jury. While his family members claimed he was not sane and was afflicted with illness, neighbors refuted those claims, instead calling Jesse a drunk. The evidence mounted against Jesse, and the jury did not take much time to return. After deliberation, lasting about forty minutes total, Jesse Ransbottom was found guilty of first-degree murder and sentenced by the judge to "hang by the neck until you are dead."

The hanging was scheduled for January 25, 1850. During the three-month period between trial and execution, repeated efforts to have Jesse's murder conviction repealed were denied. An investigation into Jesse's mental state concluded that he was not mentally insane, although he had limited mental capacity. It was determined that this limited capacity was due to poor education and bad character, and the conviction remained in place. Despite this, Jesse was convinced that the governor would commute his sentence. As carpenters began the construction of the scaffold under his jail window, Jesse gave up hope. Nervously, he watched the construction from his window day by day.

The gallows were surrounded by a fence eighteen feet high with boards planted three feet into the ground. Sawdust covered the inside ground of the eighteen-by-thirteen-foot enclosure facing Greene Street. A small stake was driven into the ground in the center of this enclosure, and a rope was attached to it. The rope ran over wheels placed in a beam overhead and down the side of the upright holding the beam. A heavy iron ball attached to the rope hung two feet above the ground as a counterweight.

When the day came to hang Jesse Ransbottom, thousands of people spilled into Xenia from all over Greene County, Montgomery County and other neighboring counties to see the first legal hanging in Greene County. When they got there, the crowd was dismayed to see the tall wooden fence surrounding the gallows and obstructing the view. Many members of the crowd had shown up on horseback and were armed. Among the crowd, rumors spread that the governor would pardon Jesse at the last moment. When the crowd gathered and saw a fence instead of gallows, more suggestions surfaced. The preeminent rumor circulating was that Jesse would be whisked away and hidden amid the chaos as he was ushered out of town and a dummy would be hanged in his place. Angry crowd members threatened to destroy the jail and hang the prisoner themselves, serving their own vigilante justice. The hanging of Jesse Ransbottom was slipping out of control before it could begin. Jesse caused as much drama with his death as he did in his life.

Mrs. William Rhoades, a neighbor occupying a nearby house, appeared at her second-story window to view the scene. Because of her vantage point, spectators below asked her to signal after the execution took place.

Mrs. Rhoades agreed to drop a white handkerchief after the drop, and the crowd was mollified.

Jesse saw just one visitor that day, his ten-year-old son. They spent several hours together before Jesse shook his son's hand and told him to tell his grandmother that he just saw his father for the last time.

As the clock struck three o'clock, the time of the execution arrived. Jesse was led out by the sheriff and the minister. He walked alone, confidently. If Jesse experienced fear, he displayed no signs of it. As he stepped on the scaffold, he stood next to the rope and calmly folded his hands over his chest. When asked, Jesse had one last thing to say, "Oh Lord! Have mercy on me. Oh, my poor mother! My poor wife! My poor children!"

The sheriff adjusted the rope and stepped back to spring the trap. Before pulling the lever, he asked Jesse if he had anything more to say. Jesse did. He asked, "Yes, will you see I am buried up yonder?"

Jesse gestured north to Champaign County. Since the sheriff had already dug a grave for Jesse, he simply said that he would see to it that Jesse was buried decently.

With the black cap pulled over his head, he folded his arms carefully over his chest. He stood calmly, waiting only for a few seconds before the sheriff pulled the lever and the trap opened, dropping Jesse to his death. Jesse dropped with a thud. The attending physician checked his watch to pronounce time of death and the rope was cut. When the crowd received signal from Mrs. Rhoades, they rushed the platform, tearing apart the wood and materials until they could see for themselves that Jesse had in fact been executed by hanging. Once satisfied, the members of the crowd dispersed.

Marked by the drop of a white cloth, the first, last and only legal hanging in Greene County concluded.

4

RIVALRY GONE SOUR

ong-standing grudges have a way of poisoning the mind. Nobody knows exactly how the grudge between laborers Andrew Kirby and John Stanton started, but on February 20, 1858, everyone saw how it ended.

Both immigrants from Ireland, Kirby and Stanton reportedly brought the grudge with them to Xenia, Ohio. Many in town had witnessed the verbal sparring between the two of them, often at the expense of Bridget Kirby, Andrew's wife. Younger and unmarried, Stanton loved to tease the older Kirby and tell him his wife was unfaithful to him with Stanton. Many others in the town reported hearing Stanton make comments declaring that he had been intimate with Mrs. Kirby. The day came when Kirby finally had enough. He went home and savagely whipped his wife, thoroughly believing her to be guilty of the allegations Stanton made against her. Afterward, Mrs. Kirby reported the assault to the police, accompanied by her son and her father. Both Mr. and Mrs. Kirby blamed Stanton for causing this incident, but for different reasons. Mr. Kirby blamed Stanton for sleeping with his wife, while Mrs. Kirby denied all accusations of cheating and blamed Stanton's teasing of her husband for causing the assault. While Kirby claimed to have caught Mrs. Kirby and John Stanton in bed together, Mrs. Kirby stated that Stanton had provoked her husband with an outrageous lie. When questioned, Stanton denied any wrongdoing and rebuffed the claim of making any comments about Mrs. Kirby to her husband or anyone else.

After the incident, Bridget Kirby and the children moved into Bellbrook with her sister-in-law, the Widow Cusick (also spelled Cusic). The Cusick home was a local gathering place for the townspeople. Liquor, especially whiskey, was sold there, and it attracted a regular crowd. Ten days later, when Kirby went to see his wife and children at the Cusick house, Mrs. Kirby refused to speak to him. He tried to grab her arm to get her to go with him, but she pulled her arm away from him. There was a large crowd at the house that night, including Stanton. Being humiliated in front of his sworn enemy must have enraged Kirby, because Kirby was seen to be watching Stanton before leaving the Cusick house. Although no words were exchanged between the two on that night, Kirby went home, sharpened his butcher knife and returned to the house, stabbing Stanton in his left side. Kirby did not remove the knife; he left it sticking out Stanton's side. Stanton removed the knife from his side and tried to stab Kirby, but Kirby fled. Kirby later commented that if there had not been such a large crowd, he might have killed Mrs. Kirby as well.

When Stanton attempted to chase after Kirby, he only made it to the porch before collapsing. People from the Cusick house carried Stanton to his home while Kirby ran away, straight to the house of Silas Hale, the justice of the peace. Kirby confessed to his crime and then begged to be hanged instead of facing the Irish, who, as he claimed, were after him. As Justice Hale went to the scene of the crime to investigate, Kirby waited at Hale's house. When Hale returned with the constable, Kirby did not resist being arrested. Kirby was placed in a jail cell Saturday night, and Stanton died of his injuries the following day. Before Stanton's death, he forgave Kirby for his murder.

The only motive Kirby would give when asked why he stabbed Stanton was that he caught Stanton in bed with his wife. Mrs. Kirby steadfastly denied the allegation, and others in town vouched for her as a trustworthy woman. Many said the real reason for the crime was the long-standing grudge between Kirby and Stanton.

The law firm of Barlow, Winans, and Corwin defended Kirby during the trial. Friends of Kirby gathered a collection to pay the former governor Thomas Corwin to defend him. Joseph A. Sexton argued for the prosecution with assistance from Loew and Gatch. On the charges of murder in the first degree, Kirby entered a plea of not guilty by reason of insanity.

During the trial, more than sixty witnesses were examined, many of whom were at the Cusick house the night of the stabbing. One of those witnesses was Silas Hale, justice of the peace. On the stand, he described the scene of the crime, the location of the house where the events took place and the time it happened. On the stand, he testified in part:

I saw Kirby the evening Stanton was killed, and suppose directly after, from what he told me. He [Kirby] came to my house and told me he had killed a man. I ask him who it was, and he said John Stanton. He came in a hurry and said he wished to give himself up to be dealt with according to law. He said the Irish were after him and would kill him....Saw Stanton, heard him say he expected to die in a short time and that Andrew Kirby had killed him. A knife was produced at the examination before me, on Tuesday. Kirby said it was his knife, that it was one with which he has worked in a slaughterhouse, and the one he had killed Stanton with.

Hale went on to describe meeting the constable at the Cusick home to see what happened while Kirby waited in a chair at his dining room table. Several witnesses told Hale they saw Kirby stab Stanton and flee the scene. Hale continued on to visit with the still-living John Stanton. Stanton told Hale that he knew his time was limited and named Kirby as his murderer. Kirby had stabbed him in the left side, leaving the knife inside. Stanton removed the knife from his side and attempted to stab Kirby, but he fled before Stanton had a chance to retaliate.

Witnesses describe Kirby's demeanor throughout the trial as calm and collected, appearing unruffled while hearing witness after witness testify against him. Despite many residents, including jurors, feeling empathy toward Kirby, it took only one week for jurors to hear all of the testimony and find him guilty of murder in the second degree, the difference between first- and second-degree murder being the premeditation of the crime. Kirby was sentenced to the penitentiary for life.

Kirby had such good behavior while he was in prison that they started to let him out during the day "to conduct business." One of the times, Kirby was late making it back to the prison before the gates were locked. While unlocking the gates the next morning, guards found Kirby lying on the ground outside the gate, waiting for it to be opened.

A Curse upon the House of Kirby

In the years following the trial and conviction of Andrew Kirby, many misfortunes struck the Kirby household. All five of the Kirby boys, Thomas, Patrick, John, William and James, enlisted to fight in the Civil War. Only four boys made it back to their mother and their sister, Catherine. Talk around town was that Andrew should be pardoned for his crime for the service and sacrifice his sons gave to our country. The pardon was denied. Andrew Kirby "went mad" in prison and was sent to the Columbus Insane Asylum to live out his years. A guardian had to be assigned to Andrew so that Mrs. Kirby could receive a pension from the son who died in war, as he had been her sole support at the time. Over the next two decades, the remaining four Kirby boys would die in separate tragedies. One died by falling under a wagon and the next three, including the youngest boy, James, died by railroad cars.

James Kirby was a conductor for the Cincinnati, Hamilton, and Dayton line of the railroad, better known as the CH&D. While attempting to walk between two railcars on the moving train, James slipped and fell between the cars onto the track and was run over by the train. He was the last of the Kirby boys to die a tragic death.

IF I CAN'T HAVE YOU...

It was late afternoon in December 1863 when a passerby heard moans emanating from the nearby cemetery. On further inspection, the passerby discovered a woman's body, face up and covered with blood and stab wounds. Near her body was a man face down, bleeding from a neck wound and barely clinging to life. The moaning had been coming from him. Though he had lost a lot of blood, doctors were able to stop the bleeding and save the man's life.

Before this untimely end, Caroline Umbenhour (also spelled Umbenhower) had been embroiled in an affair with her sister's husband, Joshua Monroe. For a brief period of time, Joshua, Umbenhour and Mrs. Monroe lived together. During this time, Monroe fathered four children with his wife and one with Umbenhour. This was not a secret affair, however, as the trio participated in the free love movement, practicing an open relationship. Umbenhour eventually moved out of her sister's house and moved in with her mother. A few months later, Umbenhour accepted a marriage proposal from another man.

Once he heard this, Monroe became agitated and asked Umbenhour to meet with him to talk. When she consented, they walked together into the cemetery at the town limits, Glen Forest Cemetery. They talked for a while and then Monroe professed his love for her, asking if she truly intended to marry her suitor. When she replied in the affirmative, his response was swift and immediate. He stabbed her in the chest and stomach several times, killing her instantly. As the adrenaline subsided and Monroe realized what he had done, he was horrified. In haste, he took his knife to his own throat, slashing quickly. Collapsing face down on the ground, his moans attracted the attention of a passerby, who summoned medical help for him.

The residents of Yellow Springs were stunned by the brutality of Monroe's actions. He was known as a docile, temperate and likeable man. Monroe was immediately imprisoned, and after a long period of recovery, he was charged with murder in the first degree by the grand jury.

Both prosecutors and the defense had no trouble finding witnesses to testify. In part, witnesses called to testify for the prosecution were:

Mrs. Abby Hildreth: Just months before her death, Umbenhour moved into her mother's house, known in the neighborhood as the Ark. Mrs. Hildreth lived a few houses from the Ark and witnessed what appeared to be Monroe making a parental visit to Umbenhour's child. As Mrs. Hildreth watched, Umbenhour and Monroe spoke at length while he visited with the child before she took the child back into the house. She also witnessed Monroe walk into the nearby alley and take clothes and a knife with him. When Umbenhour emerged from the house, he followed her down the street.

Bridget McKinney: McKinney witnessed Umbenhour and Monroe walking together into the cemetery. She was the last to see the pair before Monroe killed Umbenhour. McKinney later heard moaning and followed the sound into the cemetery, where she discovered Umbenhour and Monroe and then summoned help.

David Dunkle: Dunkle responded to the cemetery after McKinney summoned him for help. In his testimony, Dunkle confirmed the weapon, along with the description of the scene given by McKinney.

Dr. Lefevre: Dr. Lefevre was called to the scene to examine Umbenhour and Monroe after they were discovered. Dr. Lefevre counted six wounds on Umbenhour's left side and noted the blood was still warm but did not run from the wounds. He could not conclude her time of death, he said, as there was no rule to determine how long blood will flow after death. Dr. Lefevre did not see a wound on Monroe until he turned him over. Once he did, Monroe began asking if he would be transferred home. He asked several times until Dr. Lefevre asked him if there was someone with whom he wanted to speak. Monroe asked for a Mr. Lawrence, who was nearby in the growing crowd observing the scene. Monroe refused to say anything to Lawrence until the crowd dispersed, and Dr. Lefevre was able to push the crowd back a bit and then asked to stay to listen to what he told Mr. Lawrence. To the men by his side, Monroe stated that he loved Umbenhour and the child he had with her. He went on to state that Mrs. Monroe, his wife and Umbenhour's sister,

Glen Forest Cemetery, the scene of Caroline Umbenhour's death. *Author photo.*

had abused the three. Feeling troubled that day, he asked Umbenhour to talk. She consented and asked him to accompany her to a house to collect money for a sewing job she finished, but he refused and asked for a more private location. When she agreed, they walked together into the cemetery and spoke for an hour before Monroe asked her if she truly planned to marry the other man. When she replied in the affirmative, Monroe said he lost control, striking and stabbing her several times, stopping when she fell to the ground. After she hit the ground, he cut his own throat. He realized his cut was not deep enough to kill him quickly, so he stuck his hands into his wound in attempts to open it further and threw himself to the ground. It was in this state that he had been discovered. Another doctor, Dr. Thorne, came by to examine and sew Monroe's throat. Dr. Lefevre examined Umbenhour and found six of her nine stab wounds to be fatal, asserting that she could not have lived more than fifteen minutes after her attack.

Although the defense tried, they could not get the confession by proxy stricken from the record. The primary mission of the defense was to prove Monroe to be mentally unstable, as detailed by witnesses:

Mrs. Phebe Kelly was quoted to say: "I am sister to the prisoner. He always had spells of despondency. He was included to be gloomy and low spirited. At such times he never gave expressions to his feelings. He always attended to his business properly."

Rosa Monroe: Monroe's daughter. Rosa described her father as having peculiar behaviors her whole life. Her father often moved the family from one place to another. He often prayed loudly, singing and preaching to others. Other times he was silent and uncommunicative. Rosa commented that her mother was angry at the relationship between Umbenhour and Monroe. Monroe had a few bad days in the week prior to the murder, even stating he was considering moving away and starting a new life somewhere else

James Barnes: Barnes attended to the prisoner in his cell. He outlined Monroe's behavior as quiet and peaceful, only breaking his silent demeanor to sing and pray in his cell, mostly when the church bells rang. Monroe's wife took care of him until his throat wound healed.

Mrs. Barry: Mrs. Barry's husband invited Monroe to his house in the fall of 1856 to form an association for education. Since that time, Mrs. Barry observed many strange behaviors from Monroe, such as climbing to the tops of trees and sitting for hours or curling himself into a ball in a field. He often visited late at night and would announce his arrival by loudly reciting Bible passages.

When questioned about her faith, Mrs. Barry objected. Her husband was known to be a member of the free love movement, and Mrs. Barry asserted that there were many people of high morals and good judgment to believe in free love.

After closing arguments, the jury deliberated for only three hours before returning with a verdict of guilty of second-degree murder. Monroe's overall demeanor in court might have contributed to his lighter sentence, as his behavior did nothing to diminish the idea that he may be mentally unstable. During the proceedings, Monroe frequently interrupted by making wild statements and hugging the people sitting near him. Whether legitimate or fabricated, the behavior exhibited by Monroe undoubtedly had an impact on the jury's decision. All five of Monroe's children were in attendance at the trial.

With plenty of time to himself, Monroe started writing letters to the newspapers, offering explanations of his character and his perspective. In one such letter to the *Xenia Sentinel* just after his conviction, Monroe wrote a lengthy letter explaining that he was not the sort of person to harm any living creature, even stopping to prevent himself from stepping on small bugs on the ground. Monroe also mentioned the difficulty this separation was for his family but continued to say that it must be God's will. As Monroe continued in his letter, he thanked the prosecution, the sheriff, his family and many others for their kindness to him during the past year since Umbenhour's murder.

They say what goes around comes around. Less than one year into his sentence, Monroe was adjusting moving machinery when his clothes became tangled. He was pulled into the machine and mauled by the gears, dying instantly. In a matter of minutes, Joshua Monroe came to an end as violent as the one he imparted on Caroline Umbenhour.

A MOTHER'S LOVE

T he silence of the cold and snowy evening of January 11, 1867, was interrupted by a young man's screams. The young man was hysterical, shouting that a murder had taken place. Although his frenzied shouts about a terrible crime were initially doubted, the neighbors on Oak Street rushed to him. Inside the house, they discovered a gruesome scene.

Eighteen-year-old Christine Kett had been bludgeoned to death inside her home and was lying in a pool of her own blood just above the steps of the home's cellar. Her body was positioned pointing down the steps, her head and shoulders hanging over the top few steps of the cellar stairs and her lower half lying on the kitchen floor. In life, Christine Kett was undisputedly a beautiful girl. In death, she was a gruesome sight to behold. The once-beautiful young German girl had been left nearly unrecognizable. Her head had been battered into a nearly unrecognizable mass. A broken shard of her skull, matted with hair, had fallen down the cellar steps. Bits of her brain matter had spattered about the room. Her blood had spilled down the steps, collecting in a darkening pool on the floor at the bottom. Near her body lay a bloody axe and a pistol.

Christine's brother Frederick had come home from working at the home of Dr. W.W. Webster, his employer at the time. He walked into what he believed to be an empty house. After crossing through the kitchen, he discovered the gruesome scene. He then ran outside, screaming for help from his neighbors for his lifeless sister.

Doctors were called to the scene, although from what the neighbors gathered around the body could already see, it was too late for any medical intervention to help Christine. Outside, there were bloody footprints in the snow and blood smears on the fence. The pistol next to Christine's body belonged to her brother, although he said he hadn't touched it since New Year's Day, ten days before. After he fired it in the air a few times to ring in the New Year, he had separated the stock and the barrel, wrapped the parts separately then stored the wrapped pieces in the bottom of his trunk. He told police that only he and Christine knew the location of the hidden pistol.

While police examined the house and Christine's body, her mother came upon the scene. While observing the large crowd gathering outside her home, Mrs. Kett, also named Christine, became hysterical. She pushed her way through the curious onlookers, refusing all offers of comfort or condolence from her neighbors and friends as she raced to her house. When she finally pushed her way through the horde of neighbors and went into her home, she saw her daughter's body. It was at that moment her hysteria reached a dramatic peak. When she was finally subdued, Mrs. Kett told police of her whereabouts for the day and claimed she had not seen her daughter since earlier that morning. Christine had intended to go visit a friend for a few hours and then come home and prepare the evening meal.

Gunpowder had been smeared on Christine's cheeks, and she had been shot. Although there was a gunshot wound in her skull, the cause of death was not from a gunshot wound. Dr. Henry K. Steele, who had examined young Christine, described her injuries:

> *I examined Christine and found three distinct cuts on the right side of the head, two of them crossing each other at near right angles, and about four inches long each. The cut commenced about one and one-half inches above the inner angle of the right eye, running back almost to the right ear, the other at right angles to it commencing near the top of the head. The points of fracture of these cuts were burned with powder; pieces of the brains were scattered over the scalp, and the skull was fractured. The evidence of the discharge of powder proceeded obliquely forward and downward from its entrance toward the roof of the mouth. I think the pistol must have been placed close to the head and the scalp wounds made by some sharp instrument and from the amount of blood on the floor, she must have been killed before she was shot. I do not think the pistol could have been used to make the cuts in the scalp. She was not enceinte* [pregnant].

Once the excitement of discovering Christine died down, rumors circulated regarding the killer's identity. Before the Ketts had moved in, the home was a brothel. The family had constantly been harassed by rowdy men looking for a good time, unaware the home now belonged to a family. One theory was that one such rowdy man had come looking for a good time at the Kett home and assumed Christine to be a prostitute at the brothel, not realizing it was now a private residence. Christine could have grabbed her brother's gun to protect herself from an intruder. When Christine refused him, he became violent and killed her. A neighbor spotted a suspicious man, later identified as Buck Hughes, walking in the neighborhood that day. Hughes was arrested and later released after giving the police an alibi for the time of the murder. Since Christine's brother's gun was found at the scene, he was also arrested but later released after his alibi cleared. Thomas Goetz, Christine's lover, was also taken into custody and then released.

All efforts to identify the culprit of Christine's murder had failed. Despite this, Mrs. Kett continued to hurl accusations at every male who Christine encountered in her life, ranging from Christine's former suitors to random neighbors living on Oak Street. Eventually, Mrs. Kett was arrested and questioned, but she was also released.

Marshal Isaac Hale spent several months investigating Christine's death, considering every rumor. The more he dug into the case, the further he got from a resolution. After exhausting every theory, suspect and potential scenario, Marshal Hale theorized Christine must have been shooting at mice in the cellar and accidentally shot herself while tripping down the stairs. The gashes in her head, he surmised, were from hitting her head on the cellar steps as she fell backward onto the steps. Satisfied with that conclusion, Marshal Hale stopped working the case.

Although the police did not formally charge her with a crime, neighbors had already tried and convicted Mrs. Kett of Christine's murder in their minds. They could recall stories of Mrs. Kett and Christine arguing and hearing vicious threats that Mrs. Kett screamed at Christine during those times. Everyone knew she had a violent temper, and her stature was that of a woman capable of violence. A young boy from the neighborhood approached Mrs. Kett and said, "You know you killed Christy, didn't you now?"

Although that question was bluntly put across by a youth who didn't seem to remember his manners, it echoed the sentiment of the others in the German community. There may have been no formal arrest and conviction, but it was accepted as fact that Mrs. Kett killed her daughter. In the eyes of the German community, she had been found guilty. At Christine's funeral, spectators noticed Mrs. Kett did not shed a tear as she watched her daughter's coffin lowered into the ground. Many relatives and friends murmured their surprise at not receiving a confession from Mrs. Kett, as they expected the guilt would be too much to bear.

After the funeral, Mrs. Kett's health spiraled downward. She lost sleep, awakened by her own screams during the night. What little composure she once maintained, she lost as well. During screaming matches with her son, she would often threaten him with the same violence Christine suffered, assuring him he'd suffer the same fate. Her appearance became haggard as she stopped caring for herself. She moved from the house on Oak Street to another house in the city. Unable to escape the rumors and accusations in Dayton, Mrs. Kett eventually moved west to Minnesota. There she married a man named Louis Eisenstein, her fourth husband. Their marriage was short-lived and ended because Mrs. Kett was unable to get along with him. This was a pattern in her marriages, as the first two had ended the same way. Her third marriage was to John Kett, the father of her children. This marriage ended when he died after two years of service in the Civil War.

This time, Mrs. Kett moved out west, claiming to seek solace and start over. She returned to Dayton a few years later, moving to Nassau Street, near her son. Rumors died down over time, and Mrs. Kett lived a quiet life until March 1884, when she fell ill. She took to her bed with inflammation of the bowels and refused medical attention. Sensing her demise was near, she sent everyone but her son out of the room. Once everyone was gone, she handed her son the deed to the family home and told him her unspeakable secret. She was the one who killed Christine. Stunned into silence, he listened as his mother relayed her side of the story from that night in 1867.

Seventeen winters before, on that cold January day, Christine left the house to visit with a friend. Mrs. Kett told Christine to be back by noon so she could prepare the family dinner, to which Christine agreed. Although she agreed, Christine came home in the middle of the afternoon instead. Mrs. Kett was enraged. When Christine walked in the door hours later, Mrs. Kett immediately started arguing with her.

As the argument intensified, Christine turned to walk away from her mother, and Mrs. Kett picked up the nearest thing, an axe, and struck Christine in the head. Christine attempted to run away, running through the kitchen and close to the cellar before Mrs. Kett struck her in the head with the axe again. This time, Christine went down. Once the adrenaline subsided and the house quieted, Mrs. Kett felt the weight of what she had done to her only daughter. In a whirlwind of self-preservation, Mrs. Kett

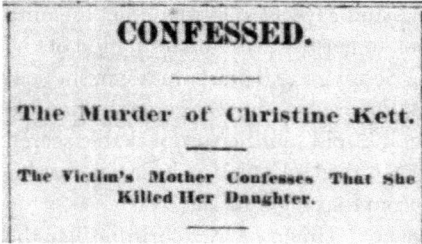

Above: After moving out West, Mrs. Kett returned to Dayton, moving into a house on Nassau Street. *Author photo.*

CONFESSED.

The Murder of Christine Kett.

The Victim's Mother Confesses That she Killed Her Daughter.

Left: Seventeen years later, Mrs. Kett confessed on her deathbed to murdering young Christine. Dayton Herald, *courtesy of newspapers.com.*

flurried about the room, removing any trace of her presence at the scene. She then searched her son's room to find his gun. When she found the gun in the trunk, she hurriedly assembled it, also grabbing a nearby flask of gunpowder. Rushing back to her daughter's mangled body, she shot the gun into her head, attempting to cover the wounds made by the axe and then hastily smeared the gunpowder on Christine's cheeks and laid the pistol by her side, in hopes that the police would see the gunshot wound and conclude that Christine had died by suicide. Mrs. Kett then fled the house and walked around downtown trying to be seen by as many people as possible to create an alibi for herself. She wandered for a few hours before coming home to the crowd gathering in front of her house. After everything died down, she was haunted by her daughter's face; she saw it everywhere. Moving houses and leaving the state didn't help, Christine's face followed her.

On March 15, 1884, unable to carry this burden any longer, she passed the weighty confession on to her son just before she died, asking him not to tell anyone what she told him until he was on his own deathbed. Although he promised his mother, he could not keep the terrible secret to himself. Instead, after what must have been an agonizing night mulling over the details of his sister's murder by their mother's hand, he let the burning secret out. Maybe he remembered all the accusations his mother made and the resulting arrests and other pieces of the puzzle that never fit. Maybe he remembered telling the police that only Christine knew where he hid his pistol and how that information led to his mother never being formally charged with Christine's murder. Perhaps he realized that his mother let him be accused and arrested for his sister's murder, all the time knowing that she did it. Whatever his thoughts were, he carried the burning secret for only one night before going to the police station. There, he told the police he could not bear the burden and lay out all the details.

Mrs. Kett is said to have been of sullen and almost vicious disposition, while in appearance she had none of the gentleness peculiar to her sex.
—Dayton Daily News

GOING OUT WITH A BANG

On a cold Christmas Eve in 1870, a boisterous crowd gathered in the upstairs game room of the American Saloon in Hamilton, Ohio. At one table, the men were playing Seven Up, a popular card game in the late nineteenth century involving memory and chance. Another table nearby hosted the card game Faro, a gambling card game so complex that the saloon employed a dealer and a watcher to keep track of the bets. Tom Myers, a well-known local gambler, was playing Faro when a group of men attacked him. It did not take long for the fight to get out of control. Through the chaos, the weapons were stones, slingshots and eventually guns. Men were throwing punches and shoving each other, and chairs and rocks were hurled. Shots rang out, partially clearing the room and calming the ruckus. When the crowd cleared and the chaos died down, Tom Myers had been shot in the side and Thomas McGehean, a former friend of Myers, was standing in the doorway.

Instantly, the suspicion fell on McGehean, as there was known to be an intense rivalry between McGehean and Myers. Witnesses came forward, claiming they had seen McGehean shoot Myers. Although Myers was reputed to be a scoundrel and tough guy, he was a well-connected tough guy. Rumors flew that the Myers family paid prosecutors to form a case against McGehean. Witness upon witness came forward, stating they had seen McGehean shoot Myers while he was kneeling on the floor, attempting to stand. Joseph Myers, brother of the victim, Tom Myers, claimed to have had spoken to McGehean just before the shooting, and he said he heard McGehean say, "Tom's my meat, upstairs, dead."

McGehean denied stating anything of the sort, and Joseph Myers did not testify to hearing this statement at trial. Another man, Jackson Garver, claimed to have seen McGehean shoot Myers in the "California Style," which means shooting at the victim through the coat without taking the gun out of the shooters pocket.

McGehean knew he was in trouble and needed a good defense lawyer. He hired renowned Dayton attorney Clement Laird Vallandigham, who had defended him previously for more minor infractions.

Vallandigham was known for more than being an attorney. He was the outspoken leader of the Copperheads in the era of the Civil War, even getting himself arrested for speaking out in support of the South. During a speech in Mount Vernon, Vallandigham declared the Civil War was fought to gain "the freedom of the blacks and the enslavement of the whites." This comment landed Vallandigham in trouble. He was brought up on a violation of General Order 38, a prohibition of sympathy for the Confederacy. After Vallandigham was convicted of his crime and sentenced, Dayton supporters of Vallandigham rioted and burned a city block, forcing President Lincoln to commute the sentence to banishment to the southern states. Vallandigham was then deported to the Confederate States of America, where he served the rest of his sentence in the form of banishment then returned to Ohio

Vallandigham and his partner Daniel Haynes had formed a legal practice that was considered to be one of the best in the West. Vallandigham was known for his meticulous attention to detail, rousing speeches, and drive to win. This drive to win overpowered any sense of morality, and he often switched sides from defense to prosecution of cases at whim. Vallandigham would only choose cases he thought he could win, and he did not care on which side of a court case he fought. Vallandigham was known for arguing his case so persuasively and ardently that the members of the jury would find themselves brought to tears by his words.

In a prior case, Vallandigham argued against a father who was arrested after a family argument with his son that turned fatal. After an intense exchange, the father lost his temper and shot his son. Sadly, the son died a short time later. Vallandigham presented a passionate and powerful argument for the prosecution against the remorseful and devastated eighty-one-year-old farmer. When the old man was ultimately convicted and then hanged for his crime, Vallandigham considered it a personal victory, with no regard for the people he left in his wake.

Trial 1: Lebanon

Jurors: Simpson Nutt, John Dunham, Charles L. Wilkerson, Eleazor Downey, J.C. Hitesman, L.H. Price, Adam B. Hathaway, Barnard Verbryke, Cephas Guttery, John Simonton, Levi Hardsock, William F. Hayner.

The hype surrounding Myers's death made it difficult to find impartial jurors who had not been reading the local newspaper articles covering the case for McGehean's trial. Thomas McGehean's first trial was moved from Hamilton Court House to the Lebanon House, currently known as the Golden Lamb.

The first trial began on June 6, 1871. Representing the prosecution was S.Z. Gard, Kelly O'Neil, S.C. Symes, M.N. McGinnis, P.H. Kohmer and George R. Sage. For the defense was Clement Laird Vallandigham, Thomas Milliken, Judge A.F. Hume, James E. Neal, Governor McBurney and Judge Wilson of Lebanon.

Under Vallandigham's detailed and deliberate questioning, witnesses contradicted themselves and disproved each other. With each new witness, Vallandigham carefully picked apart the prosecution's case, anticipating each rebuttal argument and prepared to refute any facts they gave. One witness claimed to have personally seen McGehean shoot Myers, lit by the glow of the moon from where they were standing over fifty feet away. Vallandigham went to the scene of the crime and placed himself in the spot where the witness claimed to have stood. From that vantage point, he proved the witness could not have seen what he claimed. To further his point, he cited the Farmer's Almanac, which said there had been no full moon that night, so how could any witness have seen anything illuminated by the moon on a dark night?

The case was built on the reasoning that McGehean must have had a pistol in his right pocket and shot Myers before he had a chance to get up off the floor. During the trial, Jackson Garver admitted that he was the one who grabbed Tom Myers and knocked him to the floor. Garver had also been throwing stones at Myers. Vallandigham's theory was that while Myers was being hit with stones and knocked to the floor, he reached for a weapon to defend himself from the barrage of stones coming his way. He reached for the gun inside his coat and accidentally shot himself while attempting to pull it out from the inside pocket. Vallandigham believed that either Myers's hand or the gun caught on his clothing during his haste to return fire and he accidentally pulled the trigger.

To prepare the closing argument, Vallandigham examined every detail, down to the lighting in the barroom, the visibility, what the witnesses could really have seen from where they were standing, and the physical evidence, which included the clothes Myers and McGehean wore the night of the shooting. There were no powder burns on the clothing Myers wore, and Vallandigham theorized it was because of the proximity of the gun to his clothing when it was fired. To prove his point, Vallandigham went out to a secluded area with Myers's gun and fired a few rounds into a square cloth of the same material as Myers's clothing. Vallandigham fired at the cloth from various distances to compare the bullet holes and powder burns. Once he was satisfied with this presentation of evidence, he returned to the Lebanon House to share his findings. In an excited state, he set the gun down on the table and called his fellow attorneys in to witness as he reenacted Myers's death.

Co-counsel Thomas Milliken had warned Vallandigham a few times to empty the remaining bullets from the gun to prevent any accident, since he was done testing with it. "No danger of that, I have carried and practiced with pistols too long to be afraid to have a loaded one in my pocket," Vallandigham replied confidently. "You might shoot yourself," Miliken warned. "Never fear me," Vallandigham retorted.

In his excitement, Vallandigham gathered the other attorneys, S.C. Symmes and A.J. McBurney, for the defense team. Once they were gathered, Vallandigham began his performance: "I will demonstrate to you in a moment...the absurdity of the statement that Tom Myers did NOT shoot himself." Ever the dramatic sort, Vallandigham picked up the pistol from the table, put it in his pants pocket on the right side and then continued with his speech, saying, "Now, here is the way Tom Myers had his pistol in his pocket."

During this speech, Symmes excused himself to catch up with someone walking down the hallway with whom he needed to conduct business, leaving McBurney as the sole witness to the rest of the monologue. While reenacting the brawl, Vallandigham played the role of Myers, kneeling on the floor. As McBurney watched, Vallandigham demonstrated how he surmised Myers had pulled the gun from his pocket and cocked it, standing up to demonstrate how the gun could have gone off by snagging on the material of the pants Myers wore.

Neither of the men in the room expected to hear the shot, especially not Vallandigham, who had grabbed what he assumed was the unloaded pistol from the table—only it wasn't unloaded. Intent on his climactic argument, he had carelessly set the loaded gun from his experiment on the table next to the unloaded gun he intended to use for his demonstration the next day

Sketch depicting Vallandigham accidentally killing himself. *Public domain.*

in court. Vallandigham made the wrong choice during the demonstration, carelessly picking up the loaded pistol. When he shot himself during demonstration, stunned silence filled the room. Breaking the silence was Vallandigham himself, stating, "My God, I've shot myself."

Vallandigham's remark jostled McBurney from his momentary shocked state. After that, McBurney called out for help, and people flooded the room. Several members of the counsel for both sides of the case and at least four jurors were in the room witnessing what transpired.

For the next several hours, reporters, doctors, friends and onlookers poured in, attempting to both comfort Vallandigham and witness the spectacle of his injury. Thomas McGehean himself was brought in to visit with Vallandigham, and he reportedly cried seeing Vallandigham in that state. Doctors attempted to remove the bullet, only to find that the bullet was too close to his bladder to be removed. Doctors stitched him up and laid him on his right side, and Vallandigham spent the evening vomiting. Fifty-year-old Clement Vallandigham died the next day. His ultimate cause of death was attributed to peritonitis, an inflammation of the lining of the abdominal wall that can lead to sepsis. In a tragic turn, Louisa Vallandigham, his wife, died a few weeks later. Although she had been in good health at the time of her husband's death, she deteriorated quickly once her husband died.

Vallandigham's case was built on the theory that Myers had accidentally shot and killed himself. How could he more effectively prove his client was innocent of the crime than to re-create the scenario and ultimately come to the same fate? Was this proof? In science, empirical evidence comes from results that are able to be repeated. The situation Vallandigham theorized, reconstructed and ultimately reenacted, along with the resulting bullet wound, mirrored the night in question so closely that it was impossible to believe there was any other possibility.

Shortly after Vallandigham's death, at a June 1871 meeting of the Dayton Bar, Senator Thurman delivered a rousing eulogy dedicated to the late Vallandigham, commenting in part, "No man I ever knew, or ever heard of, lost his life in so dramatic and heroic an exercise of his profession."

Although Vallandigham demonstrated his final case in the most extreme way, McGehean's first trial ended not in acquittal but rather in a hung jury. One of the twelve jurors in the first Lebanon trial, J.C. Hitesman, behaved rather suspiciously. Just before the selection of the jury, Hitesman went to the jail to visit McGehean. Sympathetically, he spoke to McGehean about his troubles. During the process of jury selection, State Attorney George Sage asked Hitesman if he had been to the jail previously to visit the prisoner.

Hitesman assured Sage that he would be impartial and judge the case fairly. Although the prosecution was concerned that Hitesman would be unfairly sympathetic, he was actually the opposite. In every deliberation, Hitesman moved to not only find McGehean guilty but hang him as well. The final result of the first trial was a hung jury. Of the other eleven jurors, four elected for manslaughter and seven wanted to acquit.

TRIAL 2: DAYTON

Jurors: John D. Crooks, Patrick Clothers, Richard Dunning, Daniel Grimes, Silvester Neff, Alex McConnell, Joseph Johnson, John Richweller, Henry Lambert, George Wright, Henry Paff and Simon Mentel.

The next trial was moved to Dayton. McGehean was tried and convicted of second-degree murder. According to McGehean, this was because many of Vallandigham's Dayton followers, known as "Vallandigbammers," were upset over his death and blamed it on McGehean's trial, unfairly influencing public opinion of McGehean. Despite the loss of a human life, McGehean described the loss of Vallandigham as "a terrible misfortune to [him] at such a critical time." On the charge of murder in the second degree, Thomas McGehean was found guilty. After the verdict, Squire Shull, John M. Sprigg and many others signed sworn affidavits alleging juryman Richweller had perjured himself when attesting that he would be fair and just while hearing the case. In these affidavits, seven in total, they swore to hearing Richweller around town declaring he knew McGehean was guilty and he would not change his mind about him. He was heard to say he would assist in the hanging of McGehean himself. When this information came to light, the verdict was overturned and a yet another new trial was granted to McGehean.

TRIAL 3: DAYTON

Jurors: Andrew Kuster, William Trumbo, Robert Sloan, Abraham Barr, Henry Gamber, William Beechler, Frank List, Amos G. Smith, Benjamin Reed, Reuben Gebhart, John S. Miller and John Eby.

During the jury selection of this trial, it was discovered that a man by the name of Mr. Thompson, father to one of Montgomery County's prosecutors, had been telling everyone in town that McGehean was guilty. Mr. Thompson owned a shop in the country just outside of Dayton and had been spreading the story of McGehean's guilt to anyone who would listen. When questioned, one man living near Thompson's store stated that he believed McGehean to be guilty. After finding out he was summoned to be a juror for the McGehean trial, he mentioned this information to Thompson, who in turn told him that McGehean was guilty. The venireman was excused from jury duty. Thompson's motive was likely to assist his son in the trial, helping him to render a guilty verdict. To avoid further issue, every man who lived near Thompson's store was dismissed without questioning. After a jury was finally selected, it took them only an hour to come back with a verdict of not guilty. Thomas McGehean was finally a free man.

Throughout the trials, McGehean's reputation had been sullied so much that he wrote a book attempting to repair his reputation and tell his side of the story. His book was titled *A History of the Life and Trials of Thomas McGehean, Who Was Charged with the Shooting and Killing of Thomas S. Myers, in the City of Hamilton, Butler County, Ohio, on the Evening of the 24th of December, 1870: Biographical Sketch of Hon. C.L. Vallandigham.* In this book, McGehean detailed at length all the times in his life he felt persecuted and wrongfully accused of crimes. He started with his early years, describing the marshal of Hamilton, John C. Elliot, as having an unprovoked grudge against him. According to McGehean, this grudge started the sullying of his reputation and the public perception that he was no good. McGehean chronicled the story of his life, blaming others for issues and incidents in each chapter. Although he stated that he wanted to show respect for the dead, McGehean could not resist throwing some jabs at Tom Myers as well. In a chapter dedicated to Myers before the shooting, McGehean gave examples of six men, three of whom he claimed were attacked and three he claimed were murdered by Myers. McGehean finished the chapter with the story of the young Pearson girl who was "ruined" by Myers "under the promise of marriage," an act Myers openly admitted to his friends that he did. As McGehean stated, when the young girl learned Myers had no intention of marrying her, she tried to convince him to do so to save her honor. As the situation continued, many others in town had learned of this issue, and Myers felt outside pressure to marry the young girl. Instead, Myers took her to his mother's house and gave her some drugs that killed her. She was then unceremoniously placed in a coffin and sent back to her relatives in Darke County. Sales of the book were credited to the many named in the book. It was rumored they bought large

Vallandigham's headstone, Woodland Cemetery. *Author photo.*

quantities of the book and burned them, hoping to prevent anyone from reading the accusations against them.

Although Thomas McGehean spoke his side in his tell-all book and had been ultimately acquitted of the crime by legal standards, many citizens opposed his presence in his home city of Hamilton, and they ran him out of town. He stayed away for a few years, taking up residence in nearby Cincinnati until the negativity died down. When he returned to Hamilton, McGehean opened a saloon. On Sunday, June 13, 1875, after drinking all day with his friends, McGehean returned to his saloon with a group to treat them to drinks at his own place. After turning on the gaslights and stepping around from the bar, McGehean received fatal gunshots.

Although the windows to his saloon were closed by the shutters, there were large diamond shapes cut out above the shutters to allow in light. It was through one of those diamond-shaped cutouts the barrel of a gun rested, aimed and awaiting McGehean's arrival. From a distance of less than six feet, McGehean received his fatal wounds in front of his friends, dying almost immediately. Although nobody claimed credit for the crime, a rumor circulating claimed colored buckshot was used as a signature in McGehean's death so someone could collect on the bounty on his head. No record has been found for anyone claiming responsibility or reward for his death.

Thomas McGehean was buried at Greenwood Cemetery in Hamilton, Ohio. Clement Vallandigham is buried at Woodland Cemetery in Dayton, Ohio. The Golden Lamb commemorates Vallandigham's place of death on the second floor. It is now a banquet hall that shares his name.

MURDER OF AN ALPHA MALE

he sleepy site of the first mill in Greene County, named Alpha after the first letter in the Greek alphabet, was rocked with excitement and scandal as news of murder spread among its residents. Although initially the news was dismissed as overinflated gossip, soon they could not deny the harsh truth. One of their beloved residents was dead.

For Charles Curry, the day had begun normally enough, heading to a picnic in the company of John "Jake" Davidson in his open buggy. The trip was a distance of roughly four miles along Alpha Road. After spending a few hours drinking and dancing with a few women at the picnic, Davidson was ready to leave. Instead of allowing his son to get back in the buggy with Davidson, Jesse Curry jumped in the cart to take his place. He told Davidson he drove the horse too fast on the way there. Jesse had noticed the erratic driving while riding behind Davidson on the way to the picnic and did not want his son in the buggy. Jesse suggested to Charles that they not ride together since Davidson was drunk. Jesse and Davidson were already arguing when they started off together in the wagon. Moments later, a scuffle ensued, and a shot rang out. Jesse Curry fell backward from the buggy onto the ground. Davidson had shot him in his left temple.

Before Jesse could hit the ground, Davidson grabbed the reins and began whipping the horses, speeding off toward Alpha. As he raced from the scene, he encountered Frank Benham in his buggy. Davidson ran his buggy into Benham's buggy, calling out to him that he had already shot one man today, and he would shoot him too. At this, he took off toward Alpha.

Meanwhile, Charles Curry, known as Charley, saw his father fall from the buggy and rushed to his side. Charley was in a buggy behind the two men accompanied by Adam Rockwell. They both plainly heard the argument between the two men and heard Davidson threaten, "I'll shoot you, where do you want it?" Charley and Rockwell then heard the explosion and saw Jesse fall from the buggy. While Charley remained with his father, Rockwell sped off toward Pushon to retrieve a doctor. Jesse Curry was taken to his home in Alpha, where he died soon after. He never regained consciousness from his fall.

After shooting his friend, Davidson fled the scene toward the home of William Cline, where he'd been living the past two years. Like an injured animal backed into a corner, Davidson fought and hissed at anyone who attempted to approach him. Constable William Fogwell led the charge to capture Davidson. Fogwell sent men to surround Davidson, and the men behind him were able to sneak up on Davidson while he was distracted talking to someone attempting to approach him directly from the front. Davidson was bound with cord and taken to jail.

At the news of Jesse Curry's death, a gloomy mood fell over the town. Jesse was regarded as a gentle and caring man. He was a veteran of the Civil War, serving in Company A of the Seventy-Fourth Regiment. Curry was severely injured in battle but was nursed back to health by his brother-in-law, Dr. Torrence. The one flaw anyone could name was that Jesse was often a drinker, as was the case on the day of his death.

Despite his actions that day, Jake Davidson was also regarded as a good guy, which made this event more surprising. Although his nature was known to be mild and sweet, he made unseemly associations which changed his life's path. The morning after the shooting, Jake made jokes in jail with the other inmates as if unbothered by his location or the events leading up to it.

A jury of "sensible, well disposed" men was assembled to hear arguments for the case. In the jury was Daniel Marshall, C.D. Ruth, James R. Lytle, Samuel McCollough, Michael Killean, Tobias Polhamus, Benjamin Kauffman, John Loo, George Funderburgh, Phillip Markley, P.H. Peterson and W.A. Conklin. For the prosecution, James E. Hawes assisted C.C. Shearer and Messers Barlow and Darlington argued for the defense. Judge Smith presided. As the court proceedings started, the stands were packed with friends of the victim eagerly waiting to hear the testimony.

The first to testify was Charles Curry, son to the victim. Charles described arriving at the picnic with Davidson, then witnessing the first argument between Davidson and his father before they left together. Davidson and Jesse Curry had started arguing over a horse when they got into the buggy together. Davidson drew a gun and then Charles attempted to calm him down by coaxing him into the buggy. At this, Jesse Curry jumped in his place, not wanting his son to ride with an angry and armed drunk man. Charles jumped into another buggy and followed the wagon.

During this pursuit, the two wagons passed each other a few times, with Davidson yelling to Charles that he would shoot him every time one wagon passed the other. Jesse Curry drove calmly, unperturbed as the wagon moved along. Eventually, Charles Curry heard Davidson ask Jesse Curry, just before shooting him, "Where will you have it?"

Curry fell from the wagon after he was shot, and Davidson took off as Charles Curry stopped his wagon to assist his father. As he sat with his father, his riding companions rode off to fetch a doctor. Curry testified that his father lived only fifteen minutes after the attack and that Davidson was drunk when the incident occurred.

William Rock was next to testify. Also a resident of Alpha, Rock rode with Charles Curry and Adam Rockwell on the day in question. Rock witnessed Davidson to be intoxicated and noted Jesse Curry was not argumentative with Davidson.

The other man riding with Rock and Charles Curry was Adam Rockwell. Rockwell corroborated the details of the shooting and described Jesse Curry as a soft-spoken man who one could not hear unless standing close to him.

William Masters drove past the wagon occupied by Curry and Davidson and saw Davidson's arm around Curry. Davidson had his gun out but kept it still, and Masters did not suspect anything wrong.

Dr. Christian Hilky saw Jesse Curry near sundown and examined him. He described a wound in the left temple, nearly one inch from the corner of the eye, backward and upward half an inch in diameter. It appeared to be a gunshot wound shot straight into the head. Two witnesses, Simon Black and Eli Trubee Sr. were there. Dr. W.H. Hagenbaugh confirmed Dr. Hilky's testimony.

Many other witnesses testified to seeing Davidson immediately after the shooting, either holding a gun or declaring he shot Curry and would do it again. These were Frank Benham, Harrison Huston, William Marony, William Huston, Joseph Grass, John Kearney, George Shank, and George Koogler.

Another man, Theodore Wingate, had spoken with Davidson two months before the shooting. During this conversation, Davidson and Wingate walked past Curry's house and Davidson remarked that he was a man he was going to kill sometime. Davidson told Wingate not to tell anyone he said that.

Hugh Jackson spoke with Davidson after the shooting. Davidson told Jackson that he shot Curry after Curry struck him.

Samuel Trubee saw Davidson after the shooting and testified he was drunk.

William Cline also testified that Davidson was drunk. Davidson told Cline that Curry struck him first.

When Davidson testified, he said he was drunk in the buggy with Curry but that he was trying to get out of the buggy and Curry would not allow him to do so. When he tried to take the reins from Curry, he struck him and told him not to do it again. Curry told Davidson he was too drunk and needed to stay in the buggy. Davidson finally had enough and wanted to get out. Davidson grabbed for the lines to stop the horses, resulting in the lines tangling in Curry's legs. Davidson said Curry threatened to break his neck, which he thought resulted in the shooting. Davidson said he could not remember exactly when he shot, but that was the moment, he supposed. Davidson denied ever telling Theodore Wingate he planned to shoot Curry.

After closing arguments from both the state and the defense, Judge Smith left the jury with explicit instructions, giving them a clear understanding of the law pertaining to the decision they were expected to make. The jury took one night to deliberate and was ready with its verdict by the next morning. After considering the evidence, John "Jake" Davidson was found guilty of murder in the second degree. Jake was later pardoned by Governor R.M. Bishop.

DYING DECLARATION

How many murder cases have the victim as the primary eyewitness? In October 1872, the city of Beavercreek was rocked by the second murder in a two-month span.

As Constable J. William Fogwell headed toward home from Dayton with a few barrels of cider in tow, he planned to stop and deliver a subpoena. As he was passing the Sumen Farm, a sudden noise from behind and to the right attracted his attention, and Fogwell turned just in time to see a flash of light and a familiar face. His mind recalled who the face belonged to as he fell backward into his wagon between the cider barrels.

Paralyzed by the bullets that struck him, Fogwell was unable to do anything but shout, "Murder! Murder!" until neighbors ran to assist him. The Sumen boys, along with Amos Harner, brought Fogwell to his father's house nearby and surgeons were summoned from nearby Xenia and Alpha to examine him. There were four wounds, one passing through the right side of his chest, one in his right arm, one in the right thigh and the fourth near his groin. Unfortunately, they concluded his recovery was nearly impossible and he would not last long.

The next morning, Fogwell was able to identify his assailant as William Ritchison. There had been bad blood between the two men for several years. Just before the shooting, Ritchison had shot several chickens and turkeys from Fogwell's farm and carried them off. Conflict between the men intensified from that day, including Ritchison threatening Fogwell's life. Fogwell told police he recognized Ritchison by his light-colored hat and butternut suit.

Fogwell had been on his way to deliver an arrest warrant to Ritchison for the shooting of his poultry. Ritchison had been alerted to this fact and was waiting for Fogwell to pass.

The mention of Ritchison's name was not the only evidence they had, however. Paper wadding was found at the spot Fogwell reported to have seen his shooter. Distinct boot prints in the ground directed a path straight to Ritchison's home, where he was calmly chopping wood as officers approached. Ritchison went quietly once he was arrested, never asking why he was being detained and showing no level of surprise at the unfolding events. While investigating his home, officers found a haversack containing a spelling book matching the wadding found at the scene. Balls in the pouch matched the bullets retrieved from Fogwell. The boots Ritchison was wearing were laid into the footprints outside and fit into the imprints as if from a mold. The pattern of the nails in the soles of the boots were close together at some points and wide apart at other points in a unique pattern. When matched with the boot prints in the ground, the nail imprints aligned perfectly.

William Fogwell lingered for several excruciating days before succumbing to his injuries. When informed of Fogwell's death, Ritchison callously remarked that Fogwell would no longer swear any more lies against him. Fogwell's funeral was large, with two thousand mourners in attendance and more than three hundred carriages in the procession.

Close in age, the two men provided a stark contrast in personalities. Both men served in the Ohio Ninety-Fourth Regiment, but while Ritchison deserted and was brought back under arrest, Fogwell served with honor. When both men returned home from service, Fogwell got married, fathered a child and was described as an honorable citizen with good character. Opposing this image was Ritchison. After being released from the service, Ritchison moved out West but moved back when he realized things weren't any better for him. He settled into a neighborhood near his father's home. During this time, Ritchison had been accused of a long list of transgressions, including petty larceny, burning haystacks and girdling apple trees. Girdling entailed cutting through the bark in a large circle around the trunk to kill the tree. The most recent offense was shooting the turkeys and chickens on Fogwell's farm.

Before the trial, Ritchison was seen before Esquire Harris, and his bail was set at $10,000. Once the trial started, the evidence and testimony piled up against Ritchison.

A man by the name of Mr. St. John testified to seeing Ritchison wearing a light-colored hat and brown coat the night of the shooting. As he continued traveling, he passed Fogwell, heading in the same direction. It was only moments later that the shooting occurred.

Reuban and Edward Suman, the brothers who ran to assist Fogwell after the shots were fired, testified to running out to his wagon and finding him between the cider barrels. With assistance from Amos Harner, they took Fogwell to his father's home, where he was examined by doctors. When Amos Harner was questioned on the stand, he recalled the statement Fogwell made when help arrived. Fogwell told the men assisting him he knew Ritchison shot him.

Also testifying was Martin Sessler, Fogwell's brother-in-law. In the early morning the day after the shooting, Sessler had been at Ritchison's house. Ritchison feigned surprise at the news of Fogwell's shooting and asked many questions, including the type of gun used and if anyone knew who did it. Ritchison snidely remarked that Fogwell had many enemies and even he himself had trouble with him. When the officers arrived to arrest Ritchison, he did not ask why he was being arrested, nor did he appear surprised. Sessler found the haversack located at Ritchison's house and a cap box roughly fifteen feet from the location of the shooting. He also grabbed Ritchison's rifle and took all the items to Fogwell's father's home and handed them to the sheriff.

Constable Jacob Harner was one of the arresting officers the day after the shooting. Deputy Sheriff Kyle faced Ritchison and stated that he was arresting him. Ritchison did not ask about charges but simply stated he would face the music. After walking out of his home, Ritchison finally asked what was happening, to which Constable Harner told him Fogwell had been shot. Ritchison told Harner he did not know Fogwell had been shot.

Sheriff W.H. Glotfelter visited the place of the shooting the next morning. While Ritchison was being arrested, Sheriff Glotfelter removed the boots Ritchison was wearing and Ritchison was given shoes to wear instead. Glotfelter took the boots and laid them in the boot prints found leading from the crime scene to Ritchison's home, and they were an exact match. Sheriff Glotfelter described the boot prints as being a mold for the boots—the match was so perfect.

Although many witnesses came forward to testify about evidence found at the crime scene matching items at Ritchison's home and many heard comments he made against Fogwell, the most damning testimony came from Fogwell himself. In a statement given to prosecuting attorney Hawes the morning after the shooting, Fogwell stated:

Yesterday I went to Dayton with a load of cider. On my return I stopped at Upper Alpha. This was about half past 6 o'clock in the evening. When I reached a point on my way home about fifteen feet or more south of the culvert, and south of Mrs. Annie Suman's house, I heard a noise in the fence corner, on the east side of the fence, and on the east, or right hand side of the road coming toward home. I thought I saw something move in the fence corner, inside of the fence; and at that moment I saw the flash of a double barreled gun. Both barrels were fired, I think, but am not positive. I immediately felt the effect of the shot in my side, which so numbed me that I fell down between the cider barrels in the wagon. I had been sitting on one of the barrels. I then hollowed "murder" four or five times and checked my horses, and heard someone running across the field, away from the fence. By the flash I saw William B Ritchison holding the gun. I am certain it was William B Ritchison whom I saw behind the fence. It was quick, but I am so familiar with his face that I am confident it was he. Think he had on a light hat and a yellowish hunting shirt or roundabout, the same color the rebels used to wear. He was standing at the fence, but I don't know whether Ritchison was immediately against the fence or not. It was very dark, about 8 o'clock, I think, when the shooting took place; but I can't tell the time certainly, I had no timepiece with me. The noise I heard in the fence corner was at the side and rear or where I was, about two rods from me, and over in the field.

I consider myself very seriously wounded; am in great misery, and suffer a great deal. I have one wound in my right shoulder; don't know where the others are, think they are in my side. I believe I shall not recover, but that I shall die of the wounds above mentioned, and I make the above statements in view of my death and at the request of Mr. Hawes, the Prosecuting Attorney.

Before closing arguments from both sides, a scandal during the trial erupted. One of the jurymen was accused of talking about the case outside the court setting. A man by the name of Elisha Ellis was out for drinks one evening in a tavern in Xenia. It was the night the jurymen were allowed to return to their family to spend an evening under the supervision of the deputy sheriff. Bar owner James Mullin testified to hearing Ellis talking about the case. He swore Ellis stated this was the worst case Xenia had ever seen and gave details of the evidence presented in the case. At one time, there were six to eight people surrounding Ellis as he recounted witness testimony and compared the case to Xenia's sensational case, the Ransbottom murder. Ellis declared Fogwell's murder to be worse than the murder of Fanny Ransbottom.

Ellis denied talking about the case. Ellis swore he simply stopped at the bar to warm up, as the weather was very cold that evening. While he sat inside getting warm, a conversation about the trial occurred at a table nearby.

Because there was an accusation of a juryman talking about the trial outside the court, an investigation ensured, further slowing the progress of Ritchison's trial. After final arguments were given on each side, it was up to Judge Smith to make a decision regarding two issues presented in the case: Fogwell's dying declaration and Ellis talking about the case.

When Judge Smith made his decision regarding these two issues, he ruled the dying declaration of Fogwell was legal and admissible as testimony. The statement was given to Reverend P.C. Prugh, who read it back to Fogwell, who then attested to the accuracy of the statement. This all took place in front of prosecuting attorney Hawes.

The other issue, juryman Ellis discussing the case, was the cause of the motion for retrial to be sustained. Under oath, James Mullin testified to the details he knew of the case from hearing Ellis talk. Judge Smith ultimately ruled that in addition to Ellis discussing the case outside the court setting, he also engaged in conversation about the case without warning people he was a juror in the case. This allowed the conversation to influence Ellis to make a decision using outside influences. Based on law, any decision rendered by a jury that included Ellis would not be valid.

Public outcry over the retrial caused the stakes to be higher for the new trial. A new jury was selected, but the trial was postponed a day to accommodate an illness. To add to the drama, a new defense team had to be assembled for Ritchison. The defense attorneys who represented him in the first trial withdrew from the case, but the Greene County court appointed them to represent him, so the county took on the expense of his defense.

An excerpt from the *Xenia Torchlight* mocking the Ellis scandal noted another juryman from the Ritchison trial stepped over a wood pile in front of his hotel. The note suggested this action might warrant a new trial as well.

Jurors had been coming and going from this case throughout both trials. Just before the first trial started, a juror was dismissed from duty when he admitted he was against capital punishment. Later, when his neighbor asked him what he suggested they do with a man who deliberately killed one of his neighbors, the expelled juryman declared, "Hang him, sir! I'd never send him up to the capital to be punished!"

Despite the bumps in the road, Ritchison was ultimately found guilty of murder in the first degree and sentenced to hang for his crime. While reading the sentencing to Ritchison, Judge Smith explained to him that there would be no escape from his sentence and told him not to expect one. He did tell him that there was one pardon he could obtain, and that was only through God's forgiveness.

But Ritchison did not want to ask God for forgiveness. Instead, he attempted to escape from custody when Deputy Sheriff Harvey Kyle was in charge of him. Kyle had been injured in the war and was missing his right arm. Ritchison thought this handicap would give him an advantage over the deputy sheriff, but he was quickly proven wrong. As Kyle was putting Ritchison into his cell, Ritchison raised his hobbled hands over his head, attempting to hit Kyle but instead hit the top of the cell door frame. This mistake was enough for Kyle to get the upper hand. The men wrestled on the floor for a bit before Kyle finally got him under control. When assistance arrived, Ritchison was shackled at hands and feet to prevent further issue.

After his thwarted escape attempt, Ritchison spent the next several days refusing to eat. Once his resolve finally broke, he asked Sheriff Glotfelter for a variety of foods, such as ice cream, watermelon and hard-boiled eggs. Glotfelter refused these foods to Ritchison, suspecting he was attempting to gorge himself as a way to eat to death. Glotfelter combated this by serving to Ritchison what he considered to be reasonable portions at each meal.

The following Saturday, Ritchison emitted an unseemly stream of profanities and announced that some people were not allowed to see the animals in their cages, referring to a recent show in town but that a caged lion would be on display the next morning.

The next morning, the meaning behind Ritchison's remark was clear. When the sheriff approached his cell, he saw something sticking out of it. On inspection, Sheriff Glotfelter discovered Ritchison's body.

Ritchison had used his bed sheets and a towel to create a rope by which to hang himself. This required significant thought, as the bar by which Ritchison hung his rope was not five feet above the ground. To remedy this issue, Ritchison raised his shackled feet as far as he could and attached the end of the makeshift rope to it, giving him more leverage for strangulation. When he was ready, he threw his feet out from under him and ended his life. Although Ritchison's neck was not broken like in a standard hanging, Ritchison appeared to have died rather quickly.

In his cell was the following letter addressed to his wife:

Dear Wife,

This night I am going to leave you a widow. Just 29 years ago today you was born, I haven't eaten a bite of anything for 15 days. I have a lot of stuff laid up to eat all at once. I want to die on a full stomach. The way is on hands and they treat me mean. Won't get me anything I have a taste for. Well I haven't suffered any yet—have a mean taste in my mouth. I am not as weak as I was the third day. There ain't anything in me but water and I do not drink a pint a day. I would have come to have seen you but as soon as I would make a long step my legs gave right away. I wish you and the children good luck. Never forget what I have told you, love. Well, now it is 7 o'clock and I have one string twisted. I have already eat more than 3 men ought to. Some try to keep good health, but I want to get sick, and I'll doctor myself if no one comes too soon. I have eat until I am in misery. I only had 9 lives, only 4 to come. Yet these people can laugh and make sport. Well, Jane, I'll try again. Harvey was here and he said that he was going to have you put on the other side. Well I want to be dead before that comes around. I can't see you get in trouble on my account. He says you handed me the saws. I told him better but he wouldn't believe me, Well I'll tell you the reason that I didn't accomplish my ends. It wasn't the intention to hurt Harvey but he came too quick and I didn't get the strings loose. At any rate, I couldn't have run, my legs were too weak. They gave right away and felt down. Well Jane, I haven't been doing right. You know that I told you I'd suffer death before I'd tell. I told Harvey the truth. He said I was too thin. I did want to see y'all, but if he do as he says, it is better for me to be dead, If I ain't read the Bible too much I'll carry it out. I hope that you may die a Christian. You have been a true woman to me, God knows. Oh! My God how could I stand it to have you crying on the other side, and have my poor sweet little babe in your arms. My hands are crossed, and I don't take my pain medicine. If they can't read it they must give it to you—I know that you can make out every word. There ain't anything shortened my days. I would have rather been dead the three weeks, and since I have found out that I haven't any strength in my legs I've been fasting so long that it has ruined me. Dear wife, I never told you who did the deed, and you know that I do know. Oh, what a pity for you and the dear little children that I didn't tell you, and then you would have made me hold on, and would have made the alarm to have frightened them. I know you wouldn't have kept

58

still like I did. Well I didn't do right, and it seems as if it is impossible for anything to come up in my favor. It is as I told you—it is death to me to tell, and death the other, so as this has went this far, let it go. I hope that I may be able to hold out. The last words I say to you are, I am innocent. Tell the children my own temper done it. Well Jane, I'll not try, for certain reasons; but Harvey said if I thought anything of my wife I'd tell her I am willing to give my life and want to die; but I ain't got anything to say. God certainly knows I want to die. I'll not write any more now. I am reduced every way but my heart; I reckon that I have nine lives. I'll not tell any more now. Well now, this is the 21st. Have two reasons that I am alive. I ain't suffering any yet. The most suffering is in my wrists, but I'll die before I ask him to take them off. My love, I'll say that you are the only one that ever did conquer me, and that was love—your lovely ways and the respect that you always showed to me, both single and married. You know that I'll stand up for those lovely smiles when you always appeared glad to see me. And if I appeared grum, then you'd kiss me to make me smile. Poor wife, if I'd known we were going to be parted, I'd have treated you to another can of oysters. Well honey, you know we certainly did live well, always had plenty to eat and loved each other—how much more can anyone have in this world. I certainly wasn't lazy, had no love for whisky but was fond of women and girls. Kiss me.

Please hand this to my wife. I'd have been dead long ago but for her lovely smile. She loved me, but when I leave her I want to die. I didn't eat anything for 15 days, and now I'll choke eight hours.

I am innocent, wife.

W.B. Ritchison.

Ritchison's father collected his body and buried him on his own farm in an unmarked grave. There was no funeral.

BEHAVE

January 17, 1880, was a normal day on the beat for patrolman Lee Lynam. During the morning, he arrested a man named John Francis under suspicion of having a gun. Not formally charged, Francis was later released and given one simple instruction: behave.

But behave, he did not.

A few hours later, at 12:15 p.m., Francis tracked Patrolman Lynam to a saloon at 109 East Third Street then shot and killed him in cold blood.

Patrolman Lynam had been a member of the force for five years and was highly regarded as one of the best men in the department. Lynam's beat was on East Third Street, and during the course of his duties, he stopped into the saloon to speak to a man by the name of George Jackson for information regarding John Francis. While he was following Jackson into the saloon, who else would appear but John Francis, following closely behind.

Francis walked into the bar, walked past Lynam and continued to the other end of the counter, which was a distance of about ten feet away. Mace Crabel, owner of the saloon and the only witness to the incident, stated that Jackson then turned to Francis, offering him a drink. Jackson later admitted that he called to Francis, offering him a drink to call attention to his presence so Lynam knew he was there. As Francis neared Jackson under the guise of taking the drink, he closed the distance between himself and Lynam by a distance of roughly eight feet. Francis then pulled out a gun, borrowed from his friend Alexander Kissinger. While Lynam

Photo of Dayton Police Department, 1876. Dayton Daily News, *courtesy of newspapers.com.*

leaned against the counter, Jackson stood behind him. Francis then drew a revolver, aimed it and shot Lynam. At the sound of the gunshot, a startled Crabel turned to the source of the noise to see Francis holding the recently fired revolver, a literal smoking gun. As he made a motion to shoot again, Jackson grabbed his arm. Francis broke free from his grasp and threatened to shoot Jackson if he interfered again. Francis then ran through the swinging doors to the back of the saloon.

Lynam threw his arms up in the air, exclaiming, "I'm shot!" He grabbed his club and started after Francis, but he quickly staggered, blood rushing from his mouth and nose. As Lynam slumped to the floor, help came to him in the form of private watchman Hatfield and officers Hughes and Grauser. Francis immediately surrendered, handing his gun over to Grauser.

During the preliminary hearing, saloon owner Mason "Mace" Crabel detailed the events of the evening. He testified that he knew both Lynam and Francis prior to the shooting and had seen them both in the bar that night. Lynam walked in first, with Francis only minutes behind. While Crabel recounted the details of Lynam's murder, the sisters and mother of Francis cried into their handkerchiefs, making significant efforts to stifle their sobs to keep order in the court.

Officer Hughes, who arrested Francis, relayed the conversation between officer and suspect before they knew Lynam had died. Officer Hughes told Francis he hoped for the sake of Lynam and for the sake of Francis that

Artist depiction of John Francis shooting patrolman Lynam. Dayton Daily News, *courtesy of newspapers.com.*

Lynam would survive the shooting. Francis replied, "For my mother's sake, I hope I have not; I shot him near the heart."

Once he had heard the testimony, Mayor Butz hesitantly declared sufficient evidence to hold Francis on the charge of first-degree murder. Once this declaration was made, the tears started in the benches. First to start was Mrs. Francis, mother of the defendant. As she buried her face into her handkerchief, shoulders shaking with sobs, her daughter sitting next to her made an attempt to comfort her. While telling her mother not to cry, she also lost control, adding to the fog of grief spreading through the courtroom. Francis made several attempts to comfort his mother, to no avail.

Before Francis was to be removed from the courtroom, Mrs. Francis, with tears streaming down her cheeks, kissed her son. Once her lips reached him, his resolve broke. It was quite the pitiable scene, watching mother, son and daughter cry. On the other side of the room, Mr. Lynam, Lee Lynam's father, was also moved to tears, although it was easy to imagine those tears were for the loss of his son and not the imprisonment of his killer.

Because Francis shot and killed a Dayton police officer, it was very difficult to obtain an unbiased jury in Montgomery County. Francis was granted a change of venue, and the trial was moved to Butler County with the Honorable Judge Alexander F. Hume presiding. The prosecution team included John Nellan, David Houk, Thomas Milliken and J.P. Young. Robert

Nevin, Esq.; Judge McKemy; Mr. Kumler; Major Blackburn; and General Van Derveer made up the defense team.

In the days before radio and television, courtroom drama and gossip were the best and most interesting forms of entertainment. Spectators packed into the courtroom, all vying to get a chance to listen to the day's proceedings. Listeners were on the edges of their seats, hanging on to every detail. During the cross-examination of the witnesses by Major Blackburn, the ticking of the clock could be heard in the dramatic pauses during arguments, enhancing the spectacle.

The prosecution had a strong case. Before shooting Lynam, Francis had spoken to several friends, making threats toward Lynam and complaining about his behavior.

First to testify was witness W.S. Hatfield, private watchman. His beat included the saloon where the crime occurred. On the stand, Hatfield corroborated the details of Crabel's story. Once Hatfield arrived on the scene, his response was to fetch a doctor to assist Lynam. Unfortunately, Hatfield was unable to get medical help to Lynam in time to save him, as Lynam expired no more than ten minutes after the initial shot was fired.

Next witness to the stand was John Johnson. Johnson had been walking down the street just before the shooting and had encountered Francis on his way to the saloon. During their conversation, Francis showed Johnson his gun and announced his intent to kill Lynam, inviting him along. Johnson then told Francis that if he was truly intending to kill a man, he wanted no part and would not accompany him to do so. Johnson then reminded him that if he were to kill a man, especially a police officer, he would either be hanged or sent to the penitentiary. They parted ways when Francis met with a woman and walked away with her. They met once more that day, and Francis confided he had been arrested earlier that morning on a concealed weapons charge but was able to dodge the charge because during the pursuit he had thrown the gun into a nearby yard before he was caught by Lynam. He later retrieved the gun after he had been released. Francis revealed his desire to shoot Lynam, but was apprehensive to do so because he thought he would be seen by other officers and shot while attempting to do so.

To bolster the premeditated angle, prosecution called another witness to the stand, James Steffin. Steffin had also spoke with Francis before the shooting regarding his intent to shoot and kill Lynam. To corroborate Johnson's story, Steffin had recounted Francis stating he would have killed Lynam long ago had he not been on the police force.

After hearing his testimony, Major Blackburn asked Steffin if he would be able to give this testimony again, word for word. Steffin said he could try and then repeated his story. When the two stories were compared, they matched almost exactly. During questioning, defense council asked Steffin if he had rehearsed or memorized his testimony, but Steffin revealed that he had been read his story several times while reviewing with prosecution before the trial.

Another witness called to the stand was William Burns. Burns also had a conversation with Francis just before the shooting. Francis told Burns of his plans to get even with Lynam. Lynam had been pursuing him, he said, and needed to be stopped.

Frank Anderson, the saloonkeeper where this conversation was held, testified to yet another conversation Francis had before shooting Lynam. Francis pulled out a gun and set it on the table in the saloon to place a bet. He changed his mind and pulled the gun off the table and placed it back in his pocket, stating he could not do without it. Before leaving, he declared Lynam would not arrest another man.

Former Dayton police officer turned night watchman Thomas Williams testified to a conversation he had with Francis in which Francis threatened Lynam's life: "I know Lynam is onto me, but if he arrests me, I am a son of a bitch if I don't kill him."

Francis continued his rant, boasting he could get Lynam any night of the week he wanted.

Ex-policeman and ex-bartender John Hinsey also had a story about Francis threatening to kill Lynam. Hinsey told Francis there would be a change in the police force and a new man, Lynam, would be assigned to the beat. Francis remarked that if Lynam ever arrested him, he would kill him.

The third bartender to testify against Francis with a similar story was Harry Keller. This time, Francis threatened a certain police officer but did not give a name. He was seen with a large knife falling out of his pocket. Keller told him he would surely get into trouble carrying that weapon around, to which Francis replied there was only one policeman with whom he held a grudge. If that officer were to arrest him, there would be trouble for him.

During this session, there were whispers of jury tampering. Rumors of a threatening letter sent to a juryman circulated until Judge Hum was able to obtain a copy of this letter and found it instead to be addressed to John Francis. This letter was from Alexander Kissinger, a close friend. The letter said:

Johnnie:
You must not weaken the least bit. We will have things our way or bust an
ass. I have one of the jurymen in good shape, and will work upon him. I
have sent to Dayton for my brother George, who has great influence with
the party that I have reference to. I will try and fix up Johnson the same as
we did Jackson today. Have courage, boy; we will do everything possible to
clear you. Please tear this up, as soon as you read it. Your ever true friend,
Alex Kiss.

After reading the letter, Judge Hume summoned for Alexander Kissinger to be brought in front of him. Once he laid eyes on "Alex Kiss," Judge Hume charged him with attempting to obstruct public justice by attempting to corrupt jurors and tampering with witnesses. With the charging of Kissinger, court was over for the day.

After this day in court, newspapers questioned whether any male inhabitants of Dayton were *not* former police officers or bartenders. They also noted that since Francis was an attractive man, there were a lot of ladies in attendance, including the wife of Judge Hume. More were expected to attend in the coming days. Defense attorney David Houk asked for stricter control on the gun in evidence during court proceedings, as he was a close and intimate friend of the late Clement L. Vallandigham, the attorney who accidentally shot himself reenacting a scenario for his client's defense. Prosecuting the case against Francis, Thomas Miliken had been a member of co-counsel for the defense of Thomas McGehean with Vallandigham on that fateful case.

When it finally came time for Francis to testify, he claimed he shot Lynam in self-defense, that Lynam cocked and pointed a gun at him immediately before Francis fired his gun. The defense team was able to provide a witness, Mr. Columbus Cathcart of Michigan. In a deposition, he swore to hearing Lynam state he would get Francis.

Defense council presented a few more witnesses who had seen altercations between Francis and Lynam. It was no secret the two men were not old friends. Both men had made threats toward each other, and both men could not meet the other on the street without having words. A few officers on the force, along with another round of bartenders, had testified to hearing arguments between the two men, and some had described Lynam as being aggressive and a bit of a bully, earning the nicknames Bull Lynam and Bully Lynam. Defense counsel had more witnesses lined up but asked the court for a delay to obtain their witnesses. The defense had dismissed several of their witnesses for the day, believing the prosecution's witness lineup would take the entire day. Once they realized the witnesses would last only the morning, Judge McKemy of the defense team asked for an adjournment. When Judge Hume denied the request, Judge McKemy cited a previous case in which the roles were reversed. During the McGehean trial, Judge Hume served as a member of the defense team, along with Milliken and Vallandigham. When Hume asked for an adjournment for the day, it was Judge McKemy who granted it. Unmoved by this request for reciprocation, Judge Hume denied the request and told defense counsel to get their witnesses back that day or they could not testify.

For sentencing, Judge Hume had Francis rise and asked him if he had anything more to say before he heard his sentence. Francis replied that he hoped Judge Hume would be lenient with him and his sentencing. In response, Judge Hume began his speech:

> *To pronounce sentence on a prisoner is always a disagreeable duty for a judge to perform. However well satisfied he may be of the prisoner's guilt, he naturally shrinks from inflicting pain upon him. Sometimes strong appeals are made to him for mercy to the prisoner that duty compels him to deny. Sometimes the very attitude of the prisoner, as he stands before him to receive sentence, helpless, oftentimes friendless, with the eyes all of fixed upon him is more touching than any words can be. Sometimes, there is something in the past life of the prisoner, in his family relations or in his present condition that excites pity for him. If he is old, his very age pleads for him. If he is young, his youth creates sympathy for him. If he is not naturally bad and vicious, but has been led into temptation and induced to commit crime by others, his weakness makes him an object of commiseration. To hold the scales of justice equally balanced under each circumstances is sometimes a difficult task.*
>
> *Strong appeals have been made to me for mercy for you. Your youth, that you have been just entered on the threshold of manhood, that you have a widowed mother who loves you, and ought to have your care as support in her declining years have been urged in your behalf. All these I have carefully considered and duly weighed.*
>
> *On the other, you have been found guilty of a heinous crime—that you have unlawfully killed a fellow-man. You have violated the law: its just demands must be satisfied. You have shown yourself to be a dangerous member of society—it must be protected against you. An example must be made that will deter others from committing like crimes.*

Certainty of punishment is in my judgment, a better preventative of crime than severity of punishment. A harsh punishment sometimes creates sympathy for a criminal and creates an unhealthy state of public opinion, while a moderate and just punishment, following speedily the commission of the crime, deters others from committing like crimes, and promotes a sound state of public opinion and satisfies its just demands.

Guided by these considerations, you are sentenced to be imprisoned in the Penitentiary of Ohio for twelve years at hard labor and to pay the cost of the prosecution.

Francis was remanded into custody and received many visitors, including ladies, during his stay. He was up for a pardon two years into his sentence but was quickly denied after public uproar in Dayton.

During his time in prison, Francis was unable to keep out of trouble. A major forgery scandal erupted, thought to have originated in the penitentiary asylum. Francis was the most likely suspect, as he had the unfettered ability to commit the crime. When questioned, Francis refused to answer any questions, so authorities resorted to extreme tactics. Francis had a penpal sweetheart while in prison. It was their intent to marry once he was released from prison. Authorities attempted to turn this woman against her love, but she refused to budge. The next resort was sending Francis to perform hard labor. He was placed in the foundry, which was the hardest work assignment. In the evenings, Francis was taken for questioning and kept until after midnight. The combination of late nights without sleep and hard manual labor appeared to break his reserve, so Francis was sent to the Annex, where he was given plenty of food and rest. Once he regained part of his strength, Francis again became defiant, so he was sent back to a routine of work duty and late nights. After six weeks of this combination, Francis was ready to talk and agreed to testify in front of the grand jury.

A few years after that, Francis wrote a letter to a friend of the late Charles "Blinky" Morgan, pretending to be Blinky. In the letter, "Blinky" claimed to be a man by the name of Charles McDonald. This caused much stress for the recipient of the letter and Blinky's other associates, as it came after Blinky had been executed for his crimes. Before the execution, Blinky had other prisoners write letters for him, including Francis, who had been the prisoner chosen to write Blinky's final statement before he was to be hanged. After writing the legitimate document, Francis wrote the false statement and sent the letter. He was known to play pranks and was immediately suspected of this cruel joke. After being released, Francis continued a life of criminal

Lynam was originally buried in an unmarked grave at Woodland Cemetery until the Dayton Fraternal Order of Police raised money for a headstone. *Author photo.*

mischief. He was arrested again in 1896 for "pocket picking." The alleged victim of this crime was a resident of the Soldier's Home, and the amount taken was $140. Francis died in 1899; the cause of death was consumption.

From a saloon floor on a cold January afternoon, forty-year-old patrolman Lee Lynam left this world and entered Dayton history as the first Dayton police officer to be killed in the line of duty. Lynam was survived by his wife, their five children, his parents and his brother. He was described as one of the best men in his department. He was buried in an unmarked grave in section 31, lot 83 at Woodland Cemetery, until 1999, when the Dayton Fraternal Order of Police raised the money and purchased him a headstone.

HARK, A MURDER BY KNIGHT

On Urbana Street in Northeast Dayton lived a woman named Catherine Hark. Sixty-five years old and a widow to Civil War veteran Adam Hart, Catherine lived off a small pension of twelve dollars a month and earned extra income by washing clothes.

Catherine, also known as Grandmother Hark, had only one daughter, named Mary Knight. Mary and Catherine did not have a good relationship, and they argued constantly. There was a long, tumultuous history between the two women, and Mary had shown a lifelong disrespect toward her mother. Mary was the type of lady who liked to stay out with "questionable companions" in bad parts of the city.

Although she settled down with her husband, a man who labored at the Brownell Boiler Plant, marriage could not settle the spirit of Mary Knight. Mary's drinking problem caused substantial hardship in her marriage, and as a result of her consistent drinking, Mr. Knight lost all the respect he had for her. After a particularly ugly argument with Mr. Knight, Mary moved from her husband's home back to her mother's home in Bitmore Commons, a neighborhood located in the far northeast corner of Dayton. Because Catherine did not have much room, she and Mary shared one bedroom and even slept in the same bed.

Mary and Catherine were different people with contrasting personalities. The only thing the ladies had in common was an appetite for strong drink. The arguments emanating between the two ladies in the next four weeks brought neighbors from their homes in attempts to pacify the screaming ladies and bring peace back to their street. The fights became commonplace, as everyday as the sound of a car passing or a bird chirping. On the morning of May 10, 1895, the shouting was louder than normal, so much so that the neighbors considered calling the police to settle the dispute. The argument continued throughout the morning. Once the yelling stopped, the neighbors saw Mary stagger from the newly silent house, undoubtedly drunk. Since this type of behavior was typical for her, nobody thought of it afterward. They forgot the incident and went about their daily business, unaware of the events to come.

Later, as neighbor Andrew Probst walked past the house, he heard Mary screaming and ran to her to see what was wrong. When asked, Mary simply pointed to the window of her home. Andrew looked in the window and saw Catherine lying on the floor with blood pooling around her. Observing her unfocused eyes, her blanched skin and the pool of blood in which she lay, Probst saw all he needed to know she was dead. Mary told Andrew he couldn't get in through the front door because it was locked, so instead he broke a window and crawled in the home to Catherine. Probst later told police that he had to assist Mary in slithering in through the window, as she was too intoxicated to get into the house without assistance.

When police arrived, Chief Farrell and Sergeant Haley pushed through the crowd of neighbors surrounding the house to find Mary sitting in a drunken stupor next to her mother, howling and moaning as she sat in a pool of her mother's blood. As Mary sat intoxicated and oblivious to her surroundings, Chief Farrell discovered the murder weapon lying next to Catherine's body. A cross piece of stovetop, which normally supported the two lids of the stove, held traces of blood and hair at its pointed edge.

At the discovery of the murder weapon, Mary snapped out of her drunken state long enough to indignantly declare her innocence to the murder. When asked to go with the police to the station to make a formal statement, Mary flailed and screamed and fought the entire way to the buggy. The neighbors divided themselves to either side of a path through which the police led the screaming Mary. As she was being shoved into the police buggy, Mary screamed to the crowd, "I'm alright now. I'm with Chief Farrell and you can't do me any harm!" Before being questioned, Mary was locked in a jail cell to calm down and regain her sobriety.

The autopsy revealed that Catherine had suffered several blows to the skull, any of which could have been the fatal strike. Multiple abrasions located at the base of Catherine's skull caused her to bleed profusely. The spike of the stove piece had cut deeply into her skull. Mary fervently denied

MURDERED.

Catharine Hark's Brains Beaten Out at Her Humble Home in North Dayton.

Mrs. Mary Knight, Her Daughter, Under Arrest, and Charged With the Crime—Both Were Drunk.

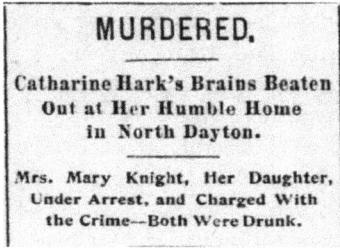

Before her trial, the public had made their mind up about Mary Knight's involvement in her mother's death. *Dayton Herald, courtesy of newspapers.com.*

any involvement in her mother's death, and when confronted with evidence, Mary had a rebuttal or an excuse for everything. The blood found on her clothing, she claimed, was from cutting her hand the previous day. She rolled up her sleeve to show an abrasion on her arm she insisted was the source of all the blood. Mary and her mother shared a bed, and the bed they slept in had no blood in it. When asked, Mary claimed she had bandaged the wound overnight and removed the dressings in the morning, which led to more bleeding. Later she added that she had also suffered a nosebleed, so that could have added to some of the blood on her dress and bonnet. Police consulted with a physician, who examined Mary and concluded she had not had a nosebleed in the past several days.

Although Mary admitted during interrogation to arguing with her mother regularly and admitted they had another argument that morning, Mary vehemently denied having ever become violent during quarrels. She simply stated she went to the corner grocery store to buy meat for their lunch. Her mother was all right when she left, and when she got back, she discovered her mother's body and a locked front door.

The next day, Chief Farrell took Mary to see her mother's body at the undertaker's parlor. Dramatically mournful, Mary sobbed and wept, holding her mother's body close to her as she wailed, "Who could have done this dreadful deed?" As she loudly wept, the coroner asked her directly if she killed her mother. To this, Mary retorted, "How could you ask such a question? I loved my mother!" Irate, Mary demanded to be set free, but instead, Chief Farrell took her back to jail.

Catherine Hark's funeral was held the next day. Pastor James Hughes of the Memorial Presbyterian Church officiated the service.

Dr. Lee Corbin, Montgomery County coroner, held an inquest the day after Catherine's funeral. Neighbors recounted damning tales of Mary's loud and sometimes violent outbursts toward her mother.

Mrs. Laura Wolf, neighbor to Mary and Catherine, was first to testify. On the day in question, she recalled seeing Mary around noon, walking down the street and weaving from side to side as she walked. Mrs. Wolf recalled that Mary appeared to be drunk. She did not see her return to her home, but a short time later, she noticed many neighbors running to the house where Mary and her mother lived. Mrs. Wolf testified to walking in the house and seeing Mary sitting on the floor next to her mother, crying and repeating that her mother was not dead. She seemed intoxicated. Mrs. Wolf continued on to name several other witnesses who had been at the crime scene that day. The witnesses were Mrs. Drapp, Mrs. Weinsteger, Mrs. Burdunder, Mrs. Seamon and Mrs. Myers, all neighbors of Catherine and Mary. Mrs. Wolf also noted the bottom pane of the front window was broken and the bloody piece of stove top on the floor next to Catherine's bloody body.

After the testimony of Mrs. Wolf, Coroner Corbin called Andrew Probst to the stand. On the stand, Probst explained that he had been walking past the house when he was alerted by Mary's calls for help. When he saw the body of Catherine Hark lying on the floor inside, he broke the front window to get into the house. He then amended the story he had originally told Chief Farrell the day of the murder. At the crime scene, Probst reported to Farrell that he helped Mary crawl through the window after he had snuck into the house. Sitting on the stand, Probst explained that he had not helped Mary crawl through the window. Instead, he explained that he crawled through the window himself then walked to the front door to let Mary walk into the house. He did not unlock the front door, he testified, as it was already unlocked when he opened it. Mary did not crawl through the window; she walked in through the front door after he opened it for her.

In the ensuing panic after the discovery of Catherine Hark's body, Mary claimed that her mother had locked the door behind her from the inside after their quarrel, forcing Andrew Probst to break a window to get into the house. It could not be determined if Probst had left the bloody print on the door when he opened it to let Mary in or if Mary had left it herself, perhaps while attempting to lock the door to give herself an alibi.

Mary was the only witness to testify in her defense. During her testimony, Mary relayed the events of the day to the coroner:

> *My name is Mary Knight. I am forty-three years old. I was born in North Dayton. I have been married for three years and have been separated from my husband for four weeks. I have been living with my mother since then. About 8:30 that morning I got twenty cents worth of whiskey from Mrs. Gantney on Valley Street. Thursday afternoon I went to Glaser's for meat and stopped in at Mrs. Weinsteger's. When I got back, I found the house locked. I supposed my mother had locked it. I went to the door after Probst*

opened it. The key was on the inside of the door. When I left the house, Mother was sitting in the doorway. I did not kill my mother. I love my mother. She is the only friend I have. I had no reason to kill her.

Despite the lack of physical evidence or motive, Mary was remanded back to jail and held until her trial two months later. No new testimony or evidence was presented at the trial, and Mary, represented by John H. Sprigg, was found guilty of the murder of her mother. Judge Dennis Dwyer denied Sprigg's appeal and sentenced Mary to one year in jail, stating, "Your conviction has been on circumstantial evidence. Let the sentence serve as atonement for the dreadful crime of which you have been found guilty."

After Mary served her sentence, her name no longer appeared in the city directory. Mary kept a low profile for the rest of her life. She died on March 1, 1903. Both Mary and Catherine are buried at Woodland Cemetery in unmarked graves.

A ROSE BY ANY OTHER NAME...

When it comes to Rose Shafor and Charles Stimmel, it's difficult to say who influenced whom into trouble. Both were getting into trouble when they found each other, and both continued getting in trouble together.

Rose Cook was born into a simple life on a farm just outside Cincinnati, and she later went from country girl to city girl after she and her family moved to Middletown. Sometime in the 1880s, the Cook family moved to Dayton, where Rose's life of crime began. Rose started getting into trouble shortly after attending school, committing acts such as "streetwalking," as the police then called it. It wasn't long until she became involved with a gang formed by her brothers, known locally as the Cook Gang. With their criminal associates, the Cook brothers had formed a gang and welcomed Rose into their fold. Police soon took notice of Rose and attempted to rescue her from her future path. She was arrested several times and given multiple small fines in attempts to deter her from her new lifestyle.

These attempts did not work. Years of mingling with criminals only further propelled Rose into her new life. If there had been any hopes of Rose straightening out her life, they were dashed when the uncommonly attractive Rose caught the attention of Charles Stimmel, also known as Dayton Slim. Stimmel was an associate of the Cook brothers, but the story of how Rose and Stimmel met is not known. What is known, however, is that Rose was no longer Rose Cook, but Rose Shafor, wife of Harry Schaeffer and mother to their son Howard. Although Rose took Harry Schaeffer's name after marriage, she decided to change the spelling for unknown reasons. Rose took Howard along when she left Harry to be with Stimmel.

The majority of the crimes Rose and Stimmel committed together were simple nonviolent jobs, such as burglaries or muggings. Although she was never caught or convicted, she was held under suspicion many times but ultimately released. It was not until the night of November 22, 1902, that the taboo relationship between Rose and Stimmel was thrust into the limelight. On that day, Dayton was shocked to learn of the robbery of Allen & Eminger's Company, a feed store located on Wayne Avenue at the railroad, and the subsequent murder of Joseph Shide, a clerk working at the store.

Joseph Shide, Harry Brush and William Fishbach were closing the shop just before supper time that day when men stormed into the shop, pistols in hand and handkerchiefs covering their faces. Terrified, Brush locked himself into an office while the masked men aimed their guns toward Fishbach and Shide. The taller masked man pointed his gun at Shide and the shorter masked man had aimed two guns directly at Fishbach. They demanded to be let into the office to get the keys to the safe. Shide and Fishbach had to call out to Brush to ask him to unlock the door, telling him the men would kill them if he didn't. Brush opened the door and ran straight out of the building. Shide and Fishbach led the masked men into the room, and as Shide stared down the barrel of a gun, he frantically fumbled through the top desk drawer, searching for a key to the safe. Fishbach stood in the corner, held in place with a gun pointed at him by the shorter man. Suddenly, a shot rang out and then another. After two loud bangs, Shide was dead on the floor, his blood pooling around him. Before running out with his partner, the taller man walked over to Shide's body and kicked him in the head several times.

Witnesses outside the feed store in the alley reported hearing gunshots then seeing men rush from the building outside into the alley and run away toward the east, disappearing from sight into the darkness of Third Street.

Immediately, suspicion fell on Stimmel, but he was nowhere to be found. Police searched for Rose as well, but she had taken her son and disappeared. They later learned Stimmel had boarded a Dayton, Springfield and Urbana traction line and headed to Springfield. Witnesses spotted a woman with a

THE FOUL MURDER OF JOSEPH SHIDE MAY YET BE AVENGED BY THE LAW

Joseph Shide, victim. Dayton Daily News, *courtesy of newspapers.com.*

young boy joining him when the car reached Findlay Street. When police questioned the friends who Rose was supposed to visit that night for dinner, they revealed that she was called out from the house by a man. Although the guests could not hear the entire conversation, they heard the man say he "had to shoot him." Together, the couple went on to Springfield and disembarked on Race Street. They procured rooms in a nearby boardinghouse. Police caught onto their movements, but Stimmel was one step ahead, leaving Rose to stay at the boardinghouse with her son while he moved on to another city. This decision may have ultimately led to his arrest.

While Rose stayed at the boardinghouse, an unexpected visitor showed up at her home. The smooth-faced and well-dressed man called himself a "picture enlarger," stating he needed to board a room. She called the landlady for him, and once the room was secured, he left, signaling to a boardinghouse across the street where two undercover policemen waited. This was no ordinary picture enlarger. This man was actually Homer Hendrickson, preeminent detective for the Dayton Police. Police chief Whitaker had sent him undercover to observe Rose more closely. Using his guise as picture enlarger, Hendrickson endeared himself to Rose, earning her trust. She opened up to him a bit about her life, mentioning a lover in Dayton. She never spoke his name, but she often referred to him as her "best boy."

For two weeks, Hendrickson had little to no information to report in his daily phone calls to Chief Whitaker. Rose was sending and receiving letters, but Hendrickson could not get a better look. Hendrickson's cover was almost blown one day when Rose's mother, Mrs. Cook, showed up at the door. Mrs. Cook and Hendrickson knew each other well, and she would have recognized him in an instant. Luckily, Hendrickson was able to hide in a pantry to avoid being seen until Mrs. Cook left.

The day finally came when Hendrickson had interesting news to report to the chief. Hendrickson saw a letter Rose was sending. Her letter was addressed to a Charles Wilson in New Orleans. Having earned her trust, Hendrickson walked with Rose into town, and she mailed the letter in his presence.

The letter reached New Orleans with more than one person eagerly awaiting its arrival. Two plainclothes policemen had positioned themselves near the pickup window so they could pounce as soon as someone picked up the letter. When that moment arrived, a man walked to the counter asking for all mail for Charles Wilson. The man asking for the letter was promptly arrested.

CHARLES STIMMEL.

Top: Stimmel's portrait as featured in the *Dayton Daily News*. *Courtesy of newspapers.com.*

Bottom: Dubbed the "Woman of Silence" by the press, Rose Shafor refused to speak for or against Stimmel. Dayton Herald, *courtesy of newspapers.com.*

Unfortunately for the police, that man was not Charles Stimmel. Stimmel suspected someone would figure out where he was staying, so he often sent others to pick up his mail while he watched from a distance. When Stimmel saw the man being arrested, not only did he leave the scene, but he fled the city as well.

Rose didn't wait long to run to her lover. She left Springfield after a few days and stopped in Dayton before fleeing to Denver to be with him. Although police could not immediately find them, they did not stop looking, and Rose and Stimmel did not let down their guard. It took several months for a break in the case, and that break came in the form of mail delivery. A tip came into the Dayton police from mailcarrier Joseph A. Hendrick. Hendrick had been delivering mail to Mrs. William Carnes, a known friend of Stimmel. Hendrick's tip led police to Denver, where Stimmel and Rose had been living as a married couple by the name of Covelly. Together they owned a horse, cow and wagon. Another dummy letter was sent to the alias, and the man arriving to pick it up was arrested.

Upon learning this information, Dayton police detectives "Bud" Neldergall and Frank McBride hurried to Denver, and one look was all it took to confirm "Dayton Slim" was the man behind bars in the Denver jail. Neldergall and McBride brought Stimmel back to Dayton to stand trial. Rose was not apprehended at the time but was picked up later.

Stimmel was returned to Dayton on August 30, 1903. Shortly after, on September 10, he was bound over to the grand jury by Squire Terry. Many came forward in hopes of getting the reward money, including Harry Brush, who was at the scene of the murder that night. Another claimed was from from John Reidy, custodian of the Federal Building in Denver, Colorado. Reidy arrested Stimmel after notification from Detectives Carberry and Sanders of Dayton, who also made a claim to the reward. The most pressing request was from Joseph Hendrick, the mail carrier. His letter read:

Dayton Ohio, Oct 21, 1904
John C. Whitaker, Chief of Police:

Dear Sir—Referring to your circular of December 5, 1902, offering $1000 reward to anyone furnishing information leading to the arrest and conviction of the man who killed Joseph W. Shide I hereby make application for said reward and base my claim upon the following statement of facts. Believing that Charles Stimmel was the guilty party and learning that he was a close friend of Mrs. William Carnes, who then lived at 1241 Wayne Avenue, which was on my mail route, I watched the mail very carefully in the belief that Stimmel would sooner or later write to her. She received various letters from points in the south, which I believed were from Stimmel. On the 18th of August, 1903, I delivered a registered letter addressed to her from Denver, Colo. The return card was addressed to Covelly. Mrs. Carnes seemed very agitated when she was asked to sign the card, denied that the letter was for her at first and by other suspicious conduct confirmed me in the belief that the letter was from Stimmel, and that he was living in Denver under the assumed name of James Covelly. I finally induced her to attach her signature to the return card by making her mark and at once reported the matter to Assistant Postmaster John V. Lytle in order that he might notify the police so that they could arrest the man who should call for the return card in Denver. Mr. Lytle did this for me and telephone your department. A detective was at once sent to him and the information was thus brought to your notice.

You gave the information to the Denver authorities and by means of it they arrested Charles Stimmel, who was convicted and punished for said crime, as you know.

Having thus furnished the information leading to the arrest and conviction of Stimmel, I am entitled to said reward, and herewith present my claim to you.

[Signed] *Joseph A Hendrick*

ATTORNEY JOHN E. EGAN,

Attorney John "Jack" Egan was fined for contempt of court for instructing Rose Shafor to refuse to speak to police. When the court appointed Stimmel a new attorney, Egan volunteered to stay on as a consultant. *Dayton Daily News, courtesy of newspapers.com.*

Back in Ohio, Rose would have been the star witness before the grand jury, but she refused to speak. Newspapers gave her the moniker "Woman of Silence." It was believed that she refused to speak on instruction from John "Jack" E. Egan, who was Stimmel's defense lawyer. Rose was confined to jail until she agreed to testify before the grand jury. Rose's son, Howard, was also brought into the grand jury room, where, like his mother, he refused to speak. He was turned over to his father, Harry, while she was jailed for contempt of court. For instructing Rose and her son, Egan was also jailed under contempt of court, and although Stimmel wanted Egan to defend him, he was appointed a new attorney.

After hearing the evidence, the grand jury indicted Stimmel on three counts of murder in the first degree.

The trial began a few months later, and undaunted by the court-appointed counsel, Egan appeared in defense of Stimmel anyway, insisting he would act as consultant and allow the court-appointed counsel, Judge Elihu Thompson and Walter Hallahan, to take the lead. After Egan was jailed and fined for contempt and Stimmel was appointed new counsel, his relatives took up a collection and rehired Egan to assist the new attorneys. Despite his claims to take a step back, he took over as independent counsel and essentially argued the entire defense on his own.

Participants in the trial included:

Defense counsel: Judge Elihu Thompson and Walter Hallahan, assisted by John Egan.
Prosecution: Judge U.S. Martin, assisted by Charles H. Kumler
Associate judge: A.W. Kumler, along with Judge O.B. Brown
Bailiff in charge of the jury: C.W. Bozenhard
Clerk of criminal court: James E. Babmer
Jury: Austin Sanger, magistrate, Madison Township; Robert Braden, retired carpenter, Van Buren Township; Charles Hoffman, farmer, Randolph

Township; George Broadrupp, florist, Harrison Township; John W. Ewry, farmer, Van Buren Township; I.T. Bassest, farmer, Harrison Township; Eli Dietrich, retired, Ohmer Park; Fergus M. Anderson, sanitary policeman, Eighth Ward; John States, retired, Fifth Ward; James Cusick, retired lightning rod agent, Brookville; John W. Watson, farmer, Jefferson Township; Charles Baker, farmer, Phillipsburg, Clay Township.

A special venire, or jury pool, of fifty-four men had been exhausted to find twelve jurors who were unbiased enough to select for trial. Immediately after selection, the jury was taken to Allen &Eminger's Feed Store to view the scene of the crime and then sequestered at the Algonquin Hotel under the direction of Bailiff Bozenhard.

Opening the trial, Judge U.S. Martin for the prosecution read the charges against Stimmel, aka Covelly, aka Lewis. Tears rolled down the cheeks of Anna Van Horn, Stimmel's mother, as she listened to the prosecutor read three charges of murder in the first degree against her son.

Martin continued on to explain the indictment from the grand jury in an opening described by the *Dayton Daily News* as "eloquent and thrilling." While his mother wept, Stimmel sat stone-faced and unmoved as he listened to the statements made against him by the prosecutor.

Weeping just a few seats over from Van Horn sat Henrietta A. Shide, Joseph Shide's mother. Joseph had been his mother's sole support in recent years, and together they had moved to Dayton from Middletown so he could get work. Next to her was her other son, Joseph's brother, Charles Shide. Charles would attend the rest of the days of the trial, but Henrietta stopped going, her nerves too worn to continue hearing about her son's death.

During the opening statement, Martin outlined the case against Stimmel, asserting he would prove Stimmel's guilt in shooting an innocent man in the back during the robbery at the feed store. He continued on to note Shide had been following every instruction Stimmel gave but still lost his life in "the least justifiable, most dastardly way, the most cowardly, and the cruelest homicide ever recorded on the annals of crime of Montgomery County."

The first witness to the stand was Stanley Sharts, deputy in the county surveyor's office. Sharts made a chart of Allen & Eminger's Feed Store, focusing on the room where the crime was committed. Through the testimony of Sharts, directions, locations, and distances were established.

Charles Eminger, proprietor of the feed store, verified Shide worked for the company for over three years and that he was a trusted employee. Only Eminger and Shide had access to the safe, which had cash in it when he left that evening. He did not remember seeing the electric light at the crossing burning when he left. This bit of information became a hotly debated issue during the trial.

During witness testimony, William Fishbach, who was the other feed store clerk, was able to explain what happened at the time of the robbery.

That night, Fishbach was on the elevator with Shide when Harry Brush beckoned to Shide. As Shide followed Brush into the office, Brush disappeared from Fishbach's sight. He then saw Shide turn and motion for Brush to come to him and the two walked into the driveway, where they were accosted by two masked men. The masked men commanded them to walk into the office and open the safe. As the men started toward the office, Brush walked ahead of them and shut himself into the office, locking the door. Shide called out to Brush, asking him to open the door or he and Fishbach would be killed. As Brush opened the doors, the rest of the men walked in, Fishbach ahead of Shide. The taller of the two masked men held one gun pointed at Shide and the shorter masked man held two, both pointed at Fishbach. The taller man then shot Shide in the leg, to which Shide cried out, "Oh, my leg!"

After this shot, Shide started toward the safe to open it for the men and the taller man fired again, this time shooting Shide in the back. After firing the fatal shot, the taller man commanded Fishbach to hand him the keys to the safe, which Fishbach did. Unable to get the safe opened, the taller man then walked over to Shide's crumpled body and removed his wallet, the whole time still covering Fishbach with his pistol. During this entire ordeal, the shorter man positioned himself next to the window, shooting nervous glances outside while also covering Fishbach with the two pistols he held.

Fishbach was also able to identify Stimmel when he saw him in court that day. In part, he testified:

> *When I was sitting in the courtroom before the preliminary trial commenced I saw Sheriff Wright bring the prisoner into the courtroom. I never knew Stimmel but when my eyes flashed on him a great conviction seized my soul. Directly in front dawned a brilliant light. It dazzled me by its superb brightness. In the center of its glow stood the figure of a man, tall and slender. My mind was forced back to the night of the murder. I recognized the man in the light as the man who covered me with a revolver and the murderer of Shide and saw that he and Stimmel were the same person. No, I never knew Stimmel before, but know positively that he is the murderer or he would not have appeared in the light.*

WILLIAM A. FISHBACH,
The Only Witness of the Murder of Joseph Shide.

William Fishbach testified that bright lights guided his identification of Charles Stimmel. Dayton Daily News, *courtesy of newspapers.com.*

"Was that a dream?" inquired Egan.

"No; a stern reality," C. Kumler replied.

As most of the courtroom was spellbound by his testimony, Fishbach continued. On further cross-examination by Egan, Fishbach stated that these lights controlled his every action in life. Any time he had a choice to make, the light would appear, guiding him to a decision. Sometimes while walking down a street, a light would appear, telling him to go a different direction down a street on his walk home. Fishbach explained that he has always followed the light but did not know of its origin and did not believe in spiritualism. He also added that though he knew Stimmel was the culprit because of his vision, he could also plainly see that Stimmel matched the basic build of the man he saw that night at the feed store.

When Harry Brush took the stand as a witness, he described the night from his perspective. As he told, Brush was finishing helping two customers and noticed Stimmel come out of the office door on Wayne Avenue. Brush knew Stimmel well, so there was no mistaking his identity. Brush watched as Stimmel joined up with another man. Seeing this, Brush ran back into the store and told Fishbach and Shide that he believed the store was about to be robbed. As he motioned for the men to come near him, he walked into the office and saw through the window that two men were in the alley tying handkerchiefs over their faces. One of the men he recognized as Stimmel. He watched as the man he said was Stimmel pushed a chair under the feed store's front door under the doorknob. At this, Brush told Shide to call the police, and Shide responded that there was no time. Before he knew it, he saw the two masked men covering Shide and Fishbach with loaded revolvers. The four men approached the side door to the office where Brush stood. Shide called out to Brush, asking him to open the door, and when he did, Brush ran outside as the four men pushed into the office. Brush described running for help at the phone office and then returning to the feed store to see Denny Madden, Frank McCain and Stimmel standing in the driveway. He saw Stimmel snap his revolver at McCain and then Brush, McCain and Madden ran out of the driveway, then he saw the two masked men rush into the alley and disappear into the darkness of Third Street. Brush noted that although McCain had a loaded revolver, the trio watched from around the corner as the masked men escaped into the darkness.

After the incident, Brush told anyone who would listen that he knew Stimmel was the culprit. He insisted he saw him in the electric lighting at the railroad crossing and he did not have a mustache that night. Brush was emphatic about that point, that Stimmel was clean shaven when he saw him in the feed store the night of the murder.

A witness statement from a Dayton saloonist said Brush and Stimmel had known each other for a long time before the feed store incident. The two men had gotten into a physical altercation, and Stimmel was the clear winner. Brush was heard to say several times and to several people that he would get even. After Hallahan broached this subject with Brush on the stand, Brush denied that he and Stimmel had any conflict anymore. Under direct questioning, Brush claimed to forget most of what he said during prior statements and testimony, even mixing up what he said about the mustache. Although the defense picked at his story, reports of the trial concluded that the defense did not damage it enough to completely discredit Brush's testimony.

Frank McCain's testimony aided the prosecution in identifying Stimmel as the culprit. McCain responded to Brush's summons for help, stopping in the driveway as a tall man pointed a gun at him. The tall man ordered him to get out, and McCain complied, forgetting the gun in his own hand. The man with him was a shorter, stockier man. When McCain saw Stimmel in the custody of McBride and Neldergall on their return from Denver, he knew Stimmel was the man he had seen the night of the feed store robbery. The electric light was burning, he noted.

Charles F. McClintoc was a machine hand at the Ohio Rake Works. He had known Harry Brush for years. McClintoc testified to witnessing the altercation between Brush and Stimmel and also stated he would not believe Brush under oath. Earl Munroe testified he knew Brush and would not believe him under oath.

Harry Webb stated he would not trust anything Brush said. He also witnessed the altercation between Stimmel and Brush at Dunley's saloon. Webb called Brush "the biggest liar on the hill."

John Lowrer was an electrician and engineer at May & Co's store. Although he didn't know Brush, he had a conversation with him in the warehouse and the furniture store. During this conversation, Brush cursed Stimmel's name and vowed to retaliate against him during the trial. This was because of the beating he took at Dunlevy's years ago.

Warren Hall's office was located a half block from Allen &Eminger's Feed Store. While outside that evening, he spotted three men standing near the railroad, standing close together and whispering. As Hall approached the men, they appeared uncomfortable, looking toward the feed store or up the track but not at him. Hall said at first, he assumed the men were railroad men and didn't think much of it. One man was tall and slim and wore a dark cutaway coat. One was shorter and stockier, wearing a black sack coat. The third was wearing a brown sack coat. Hall said that if he knew any of the men prior to that day, he would have recognized them immediately. He later commented that Stimmel was probably the same tall man he saw that night, noting he didn't think the man had a mustache, but if he did, it was a light mustache.

Frank Fogle was in Giacomino's Saloon at 6:00 p.m. the night of the murder. He met with Stimmel earlier at Third and Clinton Streets and then left him and later went to the saloon. There, he ran into Stimmel again, this time with Frank Cook.

Officer Homer Tupman was standing at Wayne and Fifth when informed of murder. He noticed the electric light was burning.

Officer Frank Ketzel also testified the light was burning that evening.

Officer William Eaton drove the patrol wagon that first reached the feed store after the murder. Once the wagon reached the feed store, Officer Clayton jumped off and Brush jumped on, stating the murderer would be caught if they drove to Third Street. Officer Eaton could not recall if the electric light was burning when he first got to the scene, but he clearly remembered it was burning after he came back from Third Street.

C.F. Young, a bookkeeper working in a factory near the railroad, was passing the feed store when he heard a shot coming from inside. He looked over in time to see a man running from the building, up the railroad track. It is presumed that this man was Brush seeking help. Young heard another shot and saw the flash of powder through the office window. Just then, two men, presumably Brush and McCain, ran back toward the store and into the driveway. Young then heard a man's voice yelling at the men. In the shadows, he could see a tall man pointing a gun at Brush and McCain as he ordered them to get back. As McCain and Brush made their retreat, Young noticed the tall man and another man walking leisurely toward Third Street. Young followed the men toward Third Street, but as he saw a patrol car speeding to the feed store, he opted instead to let the police know the direction in which he saw the men run. During cross-examination, Young admitted that he could not clearly see the faces of the men that night, and he wasn't sure if he would have recognized people he knew in that lighting.

He did believe that Stimmel matched the build of the taller man he saw the night of the robbery. Despite the lighting at the feed store, he was confident that both men were smooth faced.

E.D. Lawrence, the deputy sheriff of Clarke County, noticed a couple by the name of Charles and Rose Cook renting the home across the street from his. Living with them was a young boy named Harry. Later he learned this small family was Stimmel, Rose and her son.

On the night of November 22, 1902, Deputy Sheriff Ruppert, also from Springfield, was traveling to Carlisle to arrest a man with a warrant. As he boarded the car on the Carlisle Junction, he noticed a man and woman he knew as Charles and Rose Cook, later identified as Rose Shafor and Charles Stimmel. The pair boarded the car with a young boy. He testified that he took notice of the trio because Stimmel was so drunk that the conductor had to help him off the train. Although the conductor and Ruppert knew the description of the men from the robbery, neither of them gave the drunken passenger a second thought that night.

Another witness who spotted the trio of Stimmel, Rose and her son was Oliver Davis, motorman on the Dayton, Springfield and Urbana car that night. What stuck out to him the most was that the man of the trio was drunk, and it's generally against policy to allow inebriated passengers to board. The man was so drunk that the woman with him had to help him stand up because he could not support himself. Davis made an exception, allowing this man to board, as he had a woman and child with him, and Davis did not want to make things more difficult for them. Davis was able to positively identify Stimmel as the drunken man he saw that night, including a description of the black coat and black soft hat he wore. Davis also noted that Stimmel did not have a mustache. Despite Davis positively identifying Stimmel as the man he saw that night, he was not entirely sure about his traveling companion. He did not take as much notice of the woman who was accompanying the man, but he did believe he recognized her as Rose Shafor in the county jail.

Coroner H.H. Hatcher was the first medical witness called to the stand. Dr. Hatcher described responding to the call to the murder scene, and while examining the victim, he was told specifically that Stimmel shot and killed this man.

This statement caused a heated debate between the defense and prosecution, to which Judge Kumler threatened to adjourn court if the counsel did not calm down and resume trial. Dr. Hatcher was asked to continue his statement.

Dr. Hatcher explained Shide's cause of death, which was a hemorrhage due to the bullet striking the aortic artery. Dr. Hatcher went on to describe the path of the bullet, which struck above the heart, causing the chest cavity to fill with blood. The bullet could not have entered Shide's body while he was on the floor but instead while he was bent over, based on the path it took.

During cross-examination, Dr. Hatcher described the wounds on Shide's face, theorizing the bruising was caused by blows to the face or a fall to the floor, landing on a sharp object. Dr. Hatcher stated his call to the crime scene took place at 5:45 p.m., which caused another tiff between defense and prosecution. For prosecution, Martin asked Dr. Hatcher to explain the new concept of daylight saving time to the jury. To resolve the issue, Judge Kumler looked up the time of sunset in the almanac. "Call the man in the moon. He is the only competent witness," Martin retorted. "This almanac has a picture of a lion stirring mud!" exclaimed Charlie Kumler. "I thought I would stir you," Thompson sneered. The matter was quickly resolved by threat of the judge to adjourn court if the bickering continued.

On the stand, witness Dr. T.V. Dupuy, one of the physicians who performed Shide's autopsy, described Shide's death by bullet wound in further detail. The bullet, which came from a .32-caliber revolver, passed through the left lung, the aorta and then the right lung, severing the aortic artery. This was the cause of death, he noted. The gunshot wound to Shide's leg would not have caused his death and might not have caused him to fall to the floor but rather caused him to stoop or bend in pain. If Shide was shot in the back while stooping over, the shooter would have had to be firing from the floor. Shide had a bruise on his face, which Dr. Dupuy theorized was from falling to the floor after he was shot.

Dr. Wilfred Taylor assisted Dr. Dupuy during the autopsy and presented the bullet during trial, explaining the star-shaped pattern it made in Shide's body. Dr. Taylor was certain that the bruise on Shide's face was not caused by blows or a kick to the face, but instead a fall to the floor.

Despite a large number of witnesses, there could not be an agreement reached on the lighting situation on the night in question. Defense argued that if the electric light was not burning, then witnesses could not have clearly seen Stimmel or any other man in the darkness.

A twenty-one-year veteran to the police force, John Merkle, had been part of the response team to the scene of Shide's murder. Merkle confirmed that the electric light was on that night and had not burned out, as the defense argued.

Officer S.S. Clayton had also responded to the scene of Shide's murder that night but did not remember seeing the electric light burning. He remembered that it was rather dark when he arrived at the scene.

Frank Withoft was the superintendent of the Bertillon system, in charge of the electric lights. Withoft affirmed there were no reports of the electric light in question being out that night.

Michael Quinn was the watchman located at the railroad on Wayne Avenue. Quinn testified the light was not burning and it was too dark to recognize anyone not standing very close.

Another feed store employee, Dennis Manning, worked the afternoon of the murder but left before the robbery. He saw the electric light burning.

Homer Williams was a railroad conductor on the Pennsylvania line that ran over Wayne Avenue. He put his engine away that night around 5:00 p.m. and walked past the light on his way home. Williams noted that the light had burned out. He heard a gunshot, but it was too dark to see anything more than four feet from his face.

Frank Gustin walked past the electric light around 5:40 p.m., noting that it was blazing brightly enough to recognize a man from a distance of four hundred feet.

As an employee of the Dayton Electric Light company, Mr. Thomas's testimony corroborated Withoft's. There were no reports of this specific electric light burned out on the night in question.

Ida Holson was visiting her husband at a nearby office around the time of the robbery. A man from her husband's office announced there had been a robbery and she immediately walked outside to see but could not because it was too dark—the light was not burning.

Officer Thomas McMahon patrolled the beat where the feed store was located. While standing at Marshall and Pine Streets, he heard the shooting and pursued the suspects into the nearby lumberyard, where they were assumed to be hiding. Officer McMahon was familiar with Stimmel and had seen him around 4:30 pm. He noted Stimmel was wearing a dark slouch hat and dark cutaway coat. He was seen standing near Fifth and Clay Streets.

Bennie Stevens was certain that he saw Stimmel, Rose and her son walking east on Third Street toward Springfield Street and then to Findlay Street, where they entered Hoffman's Saloon. Rose and Stimmel drank beer until the arrival of the traction car to Springfield, and they boarded. Stevens did not believe Stimmel to be drunk and remembered a mustache on his face. Stevens alleged that he first met Stimmel that night in a saloon, and the pair had several drinks together before Stimmel left. Stevens did not see Stimmel again for about half an hour, spotting him again on Third Street near Edgar Street with Rose and her son. This sighting was approximately "two and a half squares" away from where Stimmel was seen whistling for Rose and her son to come.

Many more witnesses testified to seeing Stimmel in late November 1902, reporting to have seen Stimmel with a mustache.

John Hinnigan was a bartender for Al Sollenberger, a Springfield saloonist. Hinnigan was at his brother's place, located at 31 Limestone Street, on the night of the murder. He testified seeing Stimmel at that time painting a sign on his brother's window. He said Stimmel had a mustache but did not have an overcoat or a hat.

William McPherson was the conductor on the Dayton, Springfield and Urbana car on the night of the murder. McPherson pointed out Stimmel as the man he saw on the car that night with a woman fitting Rose's description. He noted that Stimmel wore a slouch coat, black hat and had no mustache.

William Wilson was introduced to Stimmel in late November. He remembered a mustache.

William Clark last saw Stimmel in late November 1902 and noticed Stimmel had a mustache the day in question because he had never seen him with one before. He said Stimmel was wearing a light-colored slouch hat, either gray or white.

Dora Carnes, mother of Pearl Carnes and a friend to Stimmel, spotted Stimmel and Rose in Springfield in late November. She said he had a mustache when she saw him.

Maud Snyder last spotted Stimmel in late November walking down the street with a woman. She did not recognize him until he spoke, because he had a mustache and she had never seen him with one before.

Milton Southard was a farmer living in Byhalla, near Stimmel's father. Southard met Stimmel at his father's home and remembered he had a mustache when they met.

Wayne Sullivan met Stimmel at his father's house as well. Sullivan's mother was married to Stimmel's father. Sullivan remembered seeing Stimmel with a mustache.

Mother and daughter team Margaret and Mary Brooks had known Stimmel for years and recognized him on the railroad car on the night of November 22, 1902. They both verified that Stimmel had no mustache the night they saw him on the car.

As the 1903 trial approached Christmas Day, a speedy verdict was expected to be reached. All members of the jury wanted to be home for Christmas, and the court was unable to let them take a day at home without a verdict or the direct supervision of the bailiff, who also wanted to be home for the holiday.

During closing arguments, Stimmel sat composed as prosecution denounced him, showing no reaction until he fell ill and was taken from court. Later, it was revealed that Stimmel had become sick as a result of a medication he took the previous night. More witnesses were called, but as during the trial, the witness testimonies contradicted each other, leaving more confusion for the jury.

After closing arguments were concluded, Judge Kumler instructed the jury regarding the three counts of murder against Stimmel. The first count was murder in the first degree, by which death was the intended result of the perpetrator's premeditated actions. The second count was murder in the second degree, by which the result was intended but not premeditated. The third was manslaughter, in which the intent was to harm but not kill. Judge Kumler gave a detailed explanation of the difference between the charges, explaining what circumstances must be present to convict on any of the charges.

As the jury was dismissed on Christmas Eve, they were served a Christmas Eve dinner at the Algonquin Hotel. They enjoyed the dinner, forgetting temporarily the momentous decision that lay before them. After their meal, the jury members gathered to discuss the case and make their decision. Between 7:30 and 9:40 p.m., they deliberated the fate of Charles Stimmel.

At 9:40 p.m., the tinkling of a bell broke the silence in the courtroom. It was the bell announcing the jury had reached a verdict. Spectators pushed their way in as Stimmel, his counsel and the opposing counsel found their way to their sides of the courtroom. Once they were seated, the doors to the courtroom were shut and locked so the proceedings could start.

Late Christmas Eve 1903, the twelve jurors filed into the courtroom and took their seats. Jury foreman Isaac Basset confirmed they reached a unanimous verdict, and Judge Kumler asked Chief Deputy County Clerk William H. Hosket to read the verdict. Charles Stimmel was found guilty of murder in the first degree, a sentence equaling death by electric chair. Per Judge Kumler's instructions, the jury found that:

- The defendant shot and killed Joseph Shide in Montgomery County, Ohio, at the time and location stated, in the manner and means stated.
- The killing was done purposely.

- The shooting was done maliciously.
- The shooting was done with deliberation.
- The shooting was done with premeditation.

Stimmel sat frozen as the guilty verdict hung in the air, the weight of the words lying heavily. His hands were clasped tightly, exhibiting an understated version of the emotions he felt. He displayed no other outward emotion.

As the jury read the verdict inside, Stimmel's eager paramour, Rose Shafor, waited outside to hear the news. While Stimmel awaited his fate, Rose had been released from jail. Stimmel walked back to his cell newly branded a convicted murderer while Rose stood outside flirting with Bennie Stevens.

A news reporter approached Rose and asked what she had to say about the situation. Rose retorted, "They have convicted an innocent man. I know he is innocent."

Rose then turned to leave, locking arms with her new suitor, the "sweet-scented" Bennie Stevens, as named by Stimmel's defense team. The duo walked away laughing and smiling, disappearing into the crowd as if nothing had happened.

Motions for a new trial started immediately. Egan's tactics ranged from introducing a picture of Stimmel and Rose supposedly taken at the same time the murder was committed to alleging that prime witness Harry Brush had skipped town during the trial. Egan also alleged that Stimmel was assaulted during interrogation.

The tactics did not work, and despite managing to postpone the execution date, Egan was unable to stop the execution from happening. The original date for the execution was April 19 and was then moved back to May 19 and again to July 17. After discovering that July 17 would be a Sunday, Egan was quick to move that the date be set back again. Governor Harrick was forced to grant this request, but he only granted a stay of four days. On July 21, 1904, Charles Stimmel was sent to the electric chair. Time was finally up for Dayton Slim.

In his last hours, Stimmel and Rose met one last time. Around 7:00 p.m., she visited, weeping bitterly as Stimmel sat stoic in his cell, his trademark demeanor. When Stimmel's father visited later that evening, Stimmel maintained his poise as he watched his father weep for his impending death.

Around 10:30 p.m., Stimmel summoned Chaplain Starr and gave the following statement:

Dear Chaplain—You have requested that I, Charles Stimmel, write whatever may be in my mind at the present hour. It is now 10:30. As I have but an hour and a half to live, I feel that there is a better place for me. This is a hard world and a terrific struggle and strain for us and, indeed, better at the present time since my confinement here, although I know I am going to pay the extreme penalty of the law for a crime I never had any knowledge of. All those that have wronged me and treated me unjustly, from beginning to end, will reap their reward in the future. In saying farewell, for any kindness you have shown me. I have taken your sayings under deep consideration, but have kept silent and will do what I can to save myself.

Write to Mrs. Ahlers of Dayton, whose last letter of Christian advice came this morning, and thank her for her kind and encouraging letters in her faith. Kindly remember me.

Respectfully yours,
Charles Stimmel

A short time later, Stimmel summoned for his guard, F.H. Hager, to deliver a message to his father. This message was to be kept confidential and only the three men ever knew what was said.

Just before Stimmel was to be taken to the chair, he summoned the guard one last time and handed him a piece of sharpened steel, a shank. Stimmel had created the shank from pieces of metal from a cheap tie he wore. Before handing it to the guard, Stimmel explained he kept it in case he wanted to commit suicide, but ultimately, he decided against it. To prove the sharpness of his shank, Stimmel swept it across his pants leg, producing a clean cut in the fabric.

At the stroke of midnight, it was finally the end of the line for Dayton Slim. Stimmel strolled into the tiny death room at the Ohio State Penitentiary dressed in an old black suit, underneath which he wore a colored shirt with a soiled collar and a black tie around his neck. He was smiling defiantly and smoking a cigar. On his lapel was a button imprinted with the likeness of his paramour, his Rose. His indifferent disposition wavered only slightly as his arms and legs were strapped into the electric chair and he reacted by nervously chomping on his gum. As the band connecting the contact to his shaved head was fastened under the chin, Stimmel spoke up. "Take this thing off, I have something to say," Stimmel declared. "You can talk with it on," Warden Hershey retorted.

Raising his watch up, Hershey asked the formal question of the prisoner: "Mr. Stimmel, have you anything to say before the penalty of the law is carried out?" His eyes darting around at the onlookers in the room, Stimmel began to speak. Seething with rage, he spat out the following statement: "May the curse of a dying man be on Judge Kumler, Prosecutor Martin, and his assistant, Charles Kumler, for sending me here. I never killed anyone." To Egan, who had been by his side through the entire ordeal, he said, "I thank you, Egan, for all you have done for me." To that, Egan replied that he had done everything he could do. Once Stimmel said his piece, he turned his head to Warden Hershey and spoke his last words: "Now, finish your dirty work."

Warden Hershey pushed the button, and as 1,700 volts coursed through Stimmel's body, his lanky frame jerked upward, and a loud sizzle emanated as he died. For seven seconds, this state continued, and then the voltage was turned down to 250 volts and coursed through Stimmel's body for the remainder of one minute. After a brief pause, the voltage was turned back on for a few more seconds. When Dr. J.M. Thomas, penitentiary physician, thoroughly examined Stimmel he found him to be lifeless. At 12:08 a.m., Charles Stimmel was officially dead.

Stimmel's body was laid out on the floor in front of the chair, his features smooth and even. His face took on the appearance of a man at rest, showing no signs of the punishment his body had just endured. In his pocket was a picture of Rose Shafor, the woman whose love had just cost him his life.

Stimmel's body was transported by Hibler & Riessinger, undertakers from West Dayton. To prevent a spectacle, they quickly moved Stimmel's body from Union Station into their office and locked the door. Initially, there were not many spectators, but as they day progressed, more and more onlookers tried to force their way in to see the body. The next morning after embalming, Stimmel's body was moved to 18 Morton Avenue, home of Mrs. Van Horn, Stimmel's mother.

They transported his body through Union Station. Once the train stopped moving, a woman with tears streaming down her face hastily jumped from the train, not bothering to look back. This woman was Rose Shafor. In her grief, she did not turn to see the coffin unloaded from the car as she disappeared toward Sixth Street.

As Rose approached the house, she embraced the only other woman who could understand her grief for Charles Stimmel, his mother. A reporter made a call to the house, and when he came in, he found Rose and Mrs. Van Horn crying and comforting each other. This reporter had been at the execution, and Mrs. Van Horn called on him to give her the details of her son's death. She wept silently as the reporter told her as kindly as he could about the last minutes of her son's death. Through her tears, she commented, "He died an innocent man. But even when they do find out who the guilty parties are, it will be too late to do my poor Charlie any good."

Stimmel's funeral was a private affair, with only close family and friends in attendance. Rose had stayed by Mrs. Van Horn's side through the days following his execution, and on the day of the funeral, the two clung to each other, joined by their grief. Pallbearers were Charles Watson, Arthur Schwartz, Charles Schwartz, Charles Schock and Herbert Mills. Music included the hymns "Come Ye Disconsolate" and "Rescue the Perishing." Flowers had been sent from many who wished to remain anonymous.

Stimmel was buried with a rose pinned to his lapel and a picture of Rose in his lapel pocket. Dayton Daily News, *courtesy of newspapers.com.*

Stimmel's father did not attend, later stating to the press that he had already said goodbye to his son in Columbus before the execution.

Stimmel lay in a cream-colored casket with a white rose pinned to his lapel. Next to the rose was a picture of his Rose, the same button he wore to his execution. The same picture he tucked into his pocket that day was tucked safely in his pocket again. His face held the same half smirk he used to greet the world in life, and a silky pillow billowed around his head, hiding the shaved spot from the execution. He appeared to be at peace.

Reverend J.G. Vaughn of St. Paul Methodist Episcopal Church officiated the service. He delivered a sermon preaching that the end of a physical life was not the end of the spiritual life. He closed his sermon with a poem called "I Sat Alone with My Conscience" by Charles Stubbs.

> *I sat alone with my conscience*
> *In a place where time had ceased*
> *And we talked of my former living*
> *And I felt I should have to answer*
> *The question it put to me*
> *And to face the answer and questions*
> *Throughout an eternity*
>
> *The ghosts of forgotten actions*
> *Came floating before my sight*
> *And things that I thought were dead things*
> *Were alive with a terrible might*
> *And the vision of all my past life*
> *Was an awful thing to face—*
> *In that solemnly silent place.*
>
> *And I thought of a far away warning,*
> *Of a sorrow that was to be mine,*
> *In a land that then was the future,*
> *But now is the present time;*
> *And I thought of my former thinking*
> *Of a judgment day to be;*
> *But sitting alone with my conscience*
> *Seemed judgment enough for me.*

And I wondered if there was a future
To this land beyond the grave.
But no one gave me an answer,
And no one came to save.
Then I felt that the future was present,
And the present would never go by.
For it was but the thought of my past life
Grown into eternity

Then I woke from my timely dreaming,
And the vision passed away.
And I knew the far-away warning
Was a warning of yesterday;
And I pray that I may not forget it,
In this land before the grave
That I may not cry in the future
And no one come to save

And so I have learnt a lesson
Which I ought to have known before.
And which, though I learned it dreaming,
I hope to forget no more.
So I sit alone with my conscience
In a place where the years increase,
And I try to remember the future
In the land where time will cease.
And I know of the future judgment,
How dreadful so'er it be,
That to sit alone with my conscience,
Will be judgment enough for me.

THE RETURN OF THE PRODIGAL SON

On a frozen pond near the Soldier's Home, a group of boys played a game of shimmy, an informal street hockey game. Amid the fun and competition, a stick wielded by Oliver Crook Haugh connected with another boy's face, breaking his jaw. Although it was never determined to be accidental or intentional, this incident marked the beginning of two young boys from Dayton taking wildly different paths in life.

Haugh's father had his own business, but Haugh was unsuccessful working with his family. When he took up a job at the local pharmacy, he began to self-medicate for his tooth ailments. Since Haugh's teeth were rotting and causing him a great deal of pain, he remedied this by using a combination of cocaine and intense pain relievers. Despite developing an addiction to morphine, Haugh was able to apprentice with a doctor and graduate from medical college.

After opening his first practice in 1893, Haugh declared he would find evidence of split personality, or two people living inside one body. Robert Louis Stevenson's book *The Strange Case of Dr. Jekyll and Mr. Hyde* resonated deeply with Haugh. With no small amount of self-satisfaction, Haugh declared, "I am at work on the evolution of a drug, which in its perfection will create a new era of science, a new order of thought, and a new race of beings. I will bring into the reality of day something more wonderful than Stevenson in his wildest dreams ever imagined. I will prove that which he only suggested—the certainty that two beings can exist in one body, the one blotting out the influence of the other."

Highly esteemed at the time of this declaration, Haugh settled into a home with his wife, Anna Eckley Haugh, who was happy to be married to a man she thought to be on the verge of medical innovation. Together they lived on the outskirts of town with their two children. Their happiness was short-lived, however. Anna soon discovered Haugh was secluding himself in his lab not for research but to hide the intense effects of his drug of choice, hyoscine hydrobromate.

During their marriage, Haugh's behavior continued to decline, often leading to Anna attempting to file for divorce. Throughout their relationship, she tried several times to divorce him, only to come back after he sweet-talked her or twice when she discovered she was pregnant.

As Haugh's addiction led his behavior to spiral out of control, his family had him committed to an institution, hoping he would get the help he desperately needed. Ultimately, the institutionalization did not achieve its goal, and Haugh resumed his behavior a few months later when he was released.

Once released, Haugh picked back up in his medical practice but was unable to keep patients due to his behavior while under the influence of hyoscine. Ultimately, he was forced to shut down his practice due to the deaths and serious illnesses of many patients.

Marriage did not keep Haugh from a dating life. While Haugh lived with his wife, Anna, he carried on several affairs. When a woman Haugh was dating in Toledo died under mysterious circumstances, Haugh picked up and moved to another city, repeating the pattern there as well.

Despite his marriage, the broke and jobless Haugh left Dayton, intending to open another medical practice in a city where nobody knew his name. This began a series of moves and new relationships with women, all while Haugh was still married to Anna. When things got tough for Haugh, he would simply close his practice and move to another city to start a new one. Haugh treated women mostly the same. If things got tough in his relationship, his sweetheart or anyone who caused the relationship harm would die under mysterious circumstances. Many of the deaths were suspected to be drug poisoning.

Haugh was admitted to an asylum for the second time in 1901, and once again, when released, he went back to his old habits. He continued his cycle of opening medical practices only to have them shut down due to his negligence. Haugh finally gave up and moved back to Dayton.

Once Haugh returned, his wife would not live in the same house with him, instead finally opting to file for divorce. Haugh moved back into his family home with his parents and older brother Jesse.

While in Dayton, Haugh's addiction continued to embarrass his family name, and his father finally cut him out of the will. Once he discovered this information, Haugh angrily threatened to kill his father if he was not put back into the will.

Shortly after midnight on November 5, 1905, a fire raged throughout the Haugh family home. Neighbors rushed to the scene, concerned for the welfare of the Haugh family, who they'd hoped were not inside the blaze.

Once they'd arrived, they were unable to get a clear answer from Haugh about where his family was located. Were they inside? Haugh gave vague and conflicting information, which delayed responders going into the home to rescue them. When asked directly, Haugh stated that he was in the bedroom he shared with his brother when he woke up to smoke. Although he was able to escape, his brother Jesse was trapped inside, along with his parents.

Investigation led to the discovery that Haugh had bought large quantities of hyoscine and oil before the fire. During his stays in the institutions, Haugh had been treated with hyoscine in small doses. In large doses, hyoscine has a paralyzing effect. Authorities suspected Haugh had drugged his family members before spreading oil throughout the house and setting it ablaze.

Six days later, on November 11, 1905, Haugh pled not guilty to the murder of his family. The same day, the Haugh family was laid to rest. The remains of the three adults were combined in a single casket and buried in Woodland Cemetery.

Ultimately, Haugh was convicted of the murder, despite declaring his innocence to the end. In a statement published by the *Clinton Mirror* on December 30, 1905, Haugh wrote:

> *They say I murdered my father, my mother and brother with hyoscine for the sake of the money. Then they say that when I have taken enough of the hyoscine the man within me disappears, and Hyde is the power. It seems as though I must do something—destroy something. My only recourse is to get out into the street—out into the open country—away from men and women, lest I murder them. It is possible for me to have killed these people and know nothing of it. It is possible for me to have committed all the other murders of which they accuse me, and in my normal condition be in ignorance, for in my normal condition I am another man. All that I do know is, that if I die for these crimes, I shall have at least established the proof of the theory on which I have always insisted—that two beings, one of good, the other of evil, may exist in the same man, and in that respect at least I shall have rendered a distinct service to posterity.*

Right: The remains of the Haugh family were buried together under Jacob Haugh's name. *Author photo.*

Below: Although the evidence mounted, Haugh attempted to deny all allegations of murder against him. Cincinnati Enquirer, *courtesy of newspapers.com.*

IS DR. HAUGH AN ARCHFIEND OR A VICTIM?

DR. OLIVER C. HAUGH.
Reproduced From the Only Known Photograph of the Strange Prisoner.

Dr. Haugh Being Taken From the Dayton Jail To Answer the Charge of Triple Murder.

On a frozen pond near the Soldier's Home, a group of boys played a game of shimmy. Amid the fun and competition, a stick wielded by Oliver Crook Haugh flew through the air and changed a life forever.

Haugh went on to addiction, arrests and ultimately his execution on April 19, 1907. He walked to the electric chair unassisted and was shocked only once with 1,700 volts. At 12:10 a.m., Oliver Crook Haugh was declared dead.

The other boy was an athlete with his sights on Yale but instead he was waylaid by the injuries to his face. During three long years of recovery, he was plagued with jaw pain, digestive issues, heart palpitations, and many other medical maladies. His recovery was a slow one, which gave him time to develop a fascination for science, especially aviation. Along with the help of his brother Orville, Wilbur Wright flew the first heavier-than-air flying machine on December 17, 1903.

A MURDER MOST FOWL

On a Saturday afternoon in September 1910, William Shoup heard a commotion among the chickens on his brother's farm. As he started toward the sound, he stopped and decided to go back and alert his brother, John. The two headed over to the chicken coop to investigate. As John held the shotgun, William crept over, placed one hand on each side of the door and peered into the chicken coop. He saw nothing. As the brothers walked away, they turned their attention to a cow on the farm.

William was standing just a few feet from John when he heard two shots fired. Startled, he turned toward the source of the noise in time to see a man firing the third shot, this time into his brother. The man then turned the gun on William, fired and then calmly picked up a sack of chickens that had been at his feet and walked away. Although seriously injured, William slowly recovered, and he was able to give a general description of the shooter and the clothes he was wearing.

Charles Justice was arrested by Officer Michael Graham. When confronted, Justice attempted to shoot Graham with his .38-caliber revolver. Graham was able to take it from him and get his prisoner under control. Initially, Justice complied after being arrested, but as Graham walked Justice down the road, he attempted to escape again. After walking one block, Justice stopped walking and refused to walk any more. Graham called out to another man standing in the shadows for help. When Justice saw the second man, he declared that he would go with both of them together, but not one. Under the command of the two men together, Justice walked in front of them, cursing and complaining. He then turned and spit in Officer Graham's face and broke free of their grasp. He managed to produce a knife and used it to threaten both men. It was during this time that Officer Graham shot Justice in the hip.

Justice recovered from his injury and was able to stand trial within weeks of his arrest. Long term, he recovered almost fully, with the exception of a slight limp when he walked. John Dugger, a man seen with Justice during the crime, was arrested without incident.

A coroner's inquest was called by Greene County coroner P.C. Marquart of Osborn. Fifteen witnesses were subpoenaed to appear; twenty witnesses in total testified. During the inquest, Dr. Finley testified that John Shoup's cause of death was peritonitis, a complication caused by the shooting. During surgery, the bullet was discovered in the muscle of Shoup's left side, where it came to rest after going into the right side of his abdominal cavity and passing once through the large intestine and then seven or eight times through the small intestine. The bullet was removed and matched the one removed from the chicken coop and the bullet removed from William Shoup.

A hunting party composed of Thornton Jack, Elijah Smith and Frank Crute noticed a man running toward them. In the moonlight, they could clearly see he was tall and white. As suddenly as they saw him approach, they saw him drop to the ground, his arms outstretched around his head in an apparent attempt to cover his head and face.

Another man, William Keyes, had been walking down the road at the same time. Keyes also noticed the man lying in the road. Although he didn't get a good look at the man, he saw enough to know that the man was white. Keyes walked close to him and spoke to him, but the man ignored him. Puzzled by the strange behavior, Keyes walked on a short distance and stopped again to observe the man's strange behavior. As he watched, the man picked himself up from the ground and inched along the fence line. Moments later, Keyes heard gunshots and thought to himself that Mike (Officer Michael Graham) and the man must have met.

Just after the shooting, neighbor Harry Marshall received a call informing him of the shooting. Grabbing his shotgun, he headed outside in an attempt to find the guilty party. He noticed a tall white man walking along Upper Bellbrook Road. He called out to the man, ordering him to stop. He then asked him what he was doing walking along the road at that time of day, to which the man replied that it was none of his business. After the man walked off, Marshall measured the man's tracks and reported his findings to the police. Marshall testified that he did not know Charles Justice.

At least five other witnesses testified to seeing Charles Justice and John Dugger driving away in a wagon. These testimonies corroborated the confession of John Dugger.

The other witnesses of the inquest included M.F. Burrell; police officer Michael Graham, who arrested Justice; Ephraim Spragg; Dr. W.H. Finley; Ed Muger; Brinton Hurst; R. Shank; Charles Scott; Casius A. Harner; Henry Proctor; Phillip Saunders; Mrs. Fayette Enochs; Chief of Police Smith; Dr. W.A. Galloway; Deputy Sheriff McCallister; and Ben Curl.

The findings of the coroner's inquest did not produce any new evidence, so the case was brought in front of a grand jury. Although the grand jury convened at 9:00a.m., a recess was quickly called to allow members to attend John Shoup's funeral, which started at 10:00 a.m.

A service was held at his house, conducted by Reverend Shoup of Alexandria. Directly after, another service was conducted at Zion Church. The residents of the community took time off work and time from their schedules to attend the services for their beloved friend. The mourners for both services were both so large in quantity that both the home and the church could not contain them all. In life, John Shoup was a member of the County Board of Agriculture and highly regarded as a kind husband, loving father and great friend. Reverend Shoup delivered a touching speech filled with sympathy for his friends and family.

Court proceedings were halted so members of the jury and court could attend Shoup's funeral. *Author photo.*

The grand jury considered testimony from forty-five witnesses, including many of the witnesses from the coroner's inquest. New witnesses who had not testified during the inquest were called, including Jacob Stewart, William Jeffreys and Sheriff Applegate. The grand jury required a new venire: J.S. McClure, Milton Shaw, C.K. Wolf, Charles Hook, Omer Parker, Matt Kump, John Lloyd, William Tibb, D.A. Kyle, W.A. Spahr, John Humston, Shem McDonald, J.E. Jones, C.F. Logan and William Grottendick.

Publicity of the Chicken Theft Murder created difficulty with producing an unbiased jury. Already, twelve eligible men had been used to obtain the indictment from the grand jury. For the jury of the Charles Justice trial, over one hundred men had been called. The venire, or pool of jury candidates, was especially large due to the coverage of the trial. Although a few people who had been called could not be found and a few people who were selected were dismissed to go to John's funeral, the biggest obstacle was in finding men who had not already made up their mind regarding Justice's guilt. It had been difficult to find unbiased veniremen who would listen to the evidence and make a fair assessment, perhaps even changing their minds if they had already decided. During this time, Justice sat patiently waiting, unruffled. His demeanor was described as one of a person spectating the event rather than the person on trial for murder.

After a day and a half of jury selection, twelve veniremen were finally selected: William Priest, farmer, Xenia Township; W.A. Conklin, Xenia; Brant U. Bell, farmer, Beavercreek; George L. White, merchant, Xenia; Herbert Douthett, salesman, Xenia; George Syphers, farmer, Miami Township; John A. McLain, farmer, Xenia Township; Harvey Humston, Xenia; Richard Bull, farmer, Xenia Township; Walter Laurene, farmer, Xenia Township; John B. Smith, farmer, Xenia Township; Thomas Jacobs, farmer, Miami Township.

Of all the veniremen who had been rejected for being biased, only three men were left from the original venire—Brant Bell, Thomas Jacobs and Richard Bull. For the prosecution was W.F. Orr with the assistance of Judge Marcus Shoup, cousin to John and William Shoup. Defense counsel was W.F. Trader and C.L. Maxwell, appointed by common pleas judge C.H. Kyle.

In the interim between indictment and trial, Charles Justice and John Dugger were both taken out of the city to Dayton. Authorities feared with the high publicity and intense public sentiment surrounding the case that there would be a lynch mob if they hadn't taken them out of the city. Both men received the news of the indictment with passive indifference.

During the trial, at least forty-five witnesses were called. There were no witnesses called to testify on Justice's behalf. With each witness, all attempts to paint Justice as an innocent man chipped away. As more testimony mounted against him, it became harder for the defense to deny Justice was guilty. Their attempts quickly turned from proving not guilty to getting Justice convicted of a lesser offense.

On the day of the trial, Justice walked into the courtroom with only the slightest of limps, his gait bearing but little of the injury he received during his arrest. As the indictments against him were read, Justice listened calmly and passively, as if hearing an interesting story. When asked how he plead to the murder of John Shoup, he coolly gave his reply. Not guilty.

Justice coldly repeated his apathetic answer in response to the charge of shooting with attempt to kill William Shoup. After giving his plea, he was whisked from the courtroom back to his cell. John Dugger was brought up on the same charges and pleaded the same way. Ultimately, Dugger was allowed to plead guilty to manslaughter, and he served five years in jail.

The first witness was Dr. George Anderson. Dr. Anderson testified about the nature of John Shoup's wound, recounting the details he shared during the coroner's inquest.

Next to the stand was Mrs. Bertha Black Shoup, wife of the deceased. On the stand, Mrs. Shoup testified to the events surrounding her husband's death, before and after.

The third witness was William Shoup, brother to John and the only other person who witnessed the events of John's murder. Tearfully he recounted the events of the day he lost his brother and nearly lost his own life.

Later in the evening of the shooting, liveryman Ed Thornhill hired out a rig to Charles Justice, who told Thornhill it was going to be used by John Dugger to drive to Wilmington. In all, he received a sorrel horse, a piano box buggy and a breast strap harness. Justice left the stable just after six o'clock.

Moments after the encounter with Thornhill, Dr. George Anderson of Alpha was standing at his front gate waiting for his buggy to come around front and pick him up to attend to the Shoup brothers when he noticed a covered spring wagon barreling past the home. Nearby, Albert Shank also witnessed the wagon speed past and together both men yelled at the wagon to slow down. When the wagon continued on without following his instruction, Dr. Anderson fired a few shots from his revolver in its direction.

Charles Scott met Justice at the Brinton Hurst restaurant on East Church Street and borrowed the rig from him. Scott took it for a short ride and then returned it. He did not see Justice again after that interaction. Before going separate ways, Justice told Scott he would be taking Dugger to Dayton.

Brinton Hurst's testimony was largely disregarded, as it was apparent that he was attempting to cover the fact that both Justice and Dugger were at his establishment on the night of the murder. During his time on the stand, Hurst made several wild statements on the stand, contradicting himself and the testimony of others. When pressed, he stated that he did not clearly see the driver of the wagon and could not discern whether the driver was a male or female. He did see Justice that night, he remarked, but Justice was only buying a cigar and some scrap tobacco.

Ben Curl was at the Hurst place when Dugger and Justice were there. Curl witnessed the men driving up to the Hurst place in the wagon and approaching the proprietor, Brinton Hurst. Hurst and Justice went into a back room to talk while Dugger remained outside. Curl remembered speaking to him.

After the shooting, Grant Miller was woken by a phone call alerting him of the shooting. After he hung up the phone, a man in a covered wagon approached him and asked for help with the harness. The man claimed to be paralyzed in the legs. Miller refused to help him, and the wagon resumed its journey.

Ephraim Sprigg was driving home the night of the shooting and saw two men driving the wagon. He was able to clearly see both men, and he recognized the wagon as the one formerly used by Jenkins Poultry House. Sprigg was able to easily identify the wagon, as it was briefly owned by the neighbor living across the street from Sprigg.

A fleeing man passed Charles Marchant and his father, and they patrolled the street looking for the perpetrator of the chicken coop shooting. Although they stopped him, they eventually allowed him to leave.

During trial, the details of Justice's arrest were reviewed and confirmed by H.L. Binder. Binder was the only witness present when Officer Michael Graham arrested and shot Justice.

After the last of the witnesses testified, prosecutor Orr submitted his own testimony. Orr visited Justice while he was in the county jail awaiting trial. Although most of what Justice said during this visit was not relevant to the case and subsequently the trial, he did make a useful statement. Justice refused to speak on the subject of the shooting unless he knew both men would survive their injuries. When Justice learned of Joseph Shoup's death, he refused to make any comments on the incident.

The final piece of evidence offered by the state was the dying declaration given by Joseph Shoup. Shoup stated his assailant fired the first shots while coming directly out from the chicken house before either Shoup brother had a chance to see him. The third shot fired struck Joseph Shoup.

In his final closing arguments, Judge Marcus Shoup delivered a rousing and emotional plea to the jury and courtroom. Tears spilled down many a cheek as Judge Marcus Shoup described the desolate state of a family left without a father and provider. As his dramatic speech came to a close, Judge Shoup besought the jury to return a guilty verdict "in the name of justice, for the fair name of the county; in the name of the widow and the children in the name of law, order, and decency."

After the prosecution rested, the defense presented its only evidence. Two doctors by the name of McClellan and Grube claimed the bullet that struck Shoup had first struck the shotgun in his hand and then ricocheted from the shotgun, striking his body. In their version of events, Justice and Shoup were both victims of an unfortunate turn of events.

It took thirty-five minutes for Judge Kyle to give his instructions to the jury before they could deliberate. In the carefully typed seventeen-page document he read to the jurors, Judge Kyle explained the charges that were brought against Justice and the specific laws that applied in the case. The difference between the different degrees of murder were thoroughly and clearly explained, including the finding of guilty in the first degree with or without the mercy clause. With the mercy clause in place, the defendant could be remanded to prison for life. If the defendant was found guilty of murder in the first degree without mercy, he would be sentenced to death. A conviction of murder in the first degree finds the defendant had premeditated the crime for any length of time before the act was committed, while a second-degree murder finds the death was not planned in advance.

After hearing the instructions from Judge Kyle, the jury spent just thirty-five minutes deciding.

When the jury filed back into the courtroom, three ballots were taken to determine solidarity of verdict. With the first ballot, all twelve jurymen agreed Justice was guilty of murder, with eleven believing him to be guilty of murder in the first degree and one believing it to be second degree.

A motion for a new trial was filed on two grounds. One, on the grounds that the court erred in not sustaining the challenge for cause of the defense of four jurors. Two, the verdict was manifestly against the weight of the evidence. Dismissing the motion, Judge Kyle declared there was no evidence to show the murder was not intentionally committed and that he would not set aside the guilty verdict.

The date of execution by electric chair was set for March 31, 1911. After rendering his decision, Judge Kyle had Justice rise and answer one question. "Have you anything to say why sentence should not be passed upon you by this court?" Judge Kyle demanded. "Nothing," came the solemn reply from Justice.

With a voice dripping with emotion, Judge Kyle delivered the words condemning Charles Justice to death by electrocution. Before relaying the details of the death warrant, Judge Kyle expressed sorrow that he had to be the bearer of this news: "If no higher court intervenes, and no executive clemency is extended to you, then may God have mercy on your soul."

As he recited the details of the death warrant, Judge Kyle stopped momentarily to regain his composure before he finished. Per law, Judge Kyle set the date of execution for more than one hundred days after the date of sentencing and ordered Justice be remanded to the Ohio State Penitentiary within thirty days of sentencing.

Instead of waiting, Justice was swiftly taken to the penitentiary by Sheriff McCallister and Chief of Police Smith within the hour of being sentenced. While waiting for transportation, Justice was kept in the sheriff's office in the company of several other people, including his attorneys and several courthouse officers. In that time, Justice asked his attorney if he would take up the matter of appeals with the court. To that question, W.F. Trader, his attorney, replied that they would think about it. Justice considered this answer for a moment and then nonchalantly replied, "No one need shed any tears over me. I'm not shedding any."

The rest of his time in the sheriff's office was casual, with Justice aimlessly asking about the time and when the transport would be there to take him to Columbus. He waved at a small crowd of people who had formed to watch him leave.

In the papers, Justice was painted as a man who never got a fair start in life. His mother was described as low class and she was known to have married a Black man named Joseph Helm and then divorced him and married another Black man by the name of Anderson, a huge scandal in the post–Civil War time in which Justice came of age. His mother and stepfather died in the Dayton flood of 1886, and that was the time when Justice launched himself into trouble. He spent the rest of his youth and most of his adult life in prison, having already served seven years for murder in Kingston, Canada. In his forty-eight years on earth, he had served thirty-three terms.

Most recently, he had served a twenty-year sentence for cutting his stepfather with a knife with the intent to kill. During his stay, guards discovered his work history included electrical work, so Justice was enlisted to assist in the building of "Old Sparky," the electric chair used by Ohio as a more humane alternative to hanging executions. That sentence was later commuted, and Justice was set free just a few months before the murder of Joseph Shoup. When asked about his client, attorney W.F. Trader noted that Justice never gave him any information that was helpful to his case and even denied ever being at the Shoup farm.

A stay was granted until April 28, a month after the original date. On the morning of April 28, instead of an execution, Governor Harmon granted a reprieve to Justice until June 23 to give the pardon board a chance to review his appeal. Although Justice had initially refused to assist his attorneys in his defense and subsequently his appeals, he lost his nerve. In a panic, Justice decided he wanted to extend his life in any way possible. Attorney W.F. Trader told newspapers he was considering appealing the case all the way up to the Supreme Court but hadn't come to a decision yet.

Originally, the case was appealed on two grounds. The first was the allegation that the common pleas court had erred by refusing to sustain the challenge for cause regarding four jurors John Fudge, William Conklin, John McClain and W.T. Smith. "Challenging for cause," or "strike for cause," gives attorneys permission to remove potential jurors who are unable to render a fair and unbiased decision during a trial. On the second ground, Trader alleged the jury made the decision contrary to the evidence presented. After careful consideration, Judge Alread deemed the defendant had a fair trial, noting the evidence was well connected and any jurors could have only come to one conclusion on hearing it.

Justice had no visitors until the final days, when two visitors arrived but were turned away on his request. When the day of execution came, Justice fell silent, only speaking to the guards to utter threats to their lives. The only time he did not speak to threaten was when he ordered a chicken dinner as his last meal, a final insult to the Shoup family.

Just hours before the scheduled execution, guards found a knife in Justice's cell. When pressed, Justice divulged his intent to use the knife to kill the guard responsible for cutting his slacks to attach the electrodes. After a failed escape attempt, Justice accused the two prisoners confined with him of blabbing to the guards and getting him caught. When he directed his murderous threats toward them, Justice was separated from the others.

Thirteen months after the murder of Joseph Shoup and seven stays of execution later, Justice was finally put to death on October 27, 1911. His walk to the chair was stoic and unperturbed, as if he was merely walking from one room to another. Witnesses present included Sheriff McCallister, Dr. George Anderson and Al Zeiner. When asked if he had any last words, Justice simply stated, "I am not guilty of the crime for which you are killing me."

Justice did not remain long enough to hear a response to his statement; his words died on his lips. In the electric chair he helped build, Justice was served.

MURDER. STOP.

When Louis E. Parker's wife of nine years, Lalor, ran away from Savannah, Georgia, to be with her lover, Chestnut Payne, Parker was confident she would come back. This was not the first time she had run away. The first time she ran away with Chestnut, known as Chester, was just a few months before, and it was under the guise of going away for work. Lalor and Payne went to Cincinnati but came back to Savannah after a few weeks. This time, she moved into a house at 360 Cincinnati Street with Payne and moved in her mother; her fourteen-year-old daughter, Lucille, from a previous relationship, a common law marriage; and her son with Parker, eight-year-old Louis Jr., nicknamed Sunshine. Parker wasn't concerned. When Lalor left him and ran away just months before, she worked for a few weeks and then returned. She was with Payne at that time as well and she had returned. Because of that, Parker thought she would return this time too.

The plan was simple. Parker would follow his wife to Ohio, reconcile their marriage and bring her and the kids back home for Christmas. The family would be together in just a few days, and this would be the last time she left him—she wouldn't run off again. All they had to do was reconcile. On December 22, 1934, he quit his job as a Savannah motorcycle cop and headed north.

A day later, when Parker finally caught up to his wife and her lover, they were in Dayton, Ohio. He rented a room for the night, signing in as Dave Jones, seaman. The next day, Christmas Eve, Louis sent a telegram to his wife, hoping to meet her at the postal office located at Third and Ludlow Streets. To entice her to show up, he added ten dollars. Surely, she would show to get the money. Parker thought that if he could get her to the postal telegraph office, he could reconcile with her in person. While he waited, Louis walked across the street to the Dayton Arcade to get his shoes shined and wait for his wife to arrive.

To his dismay, Lalor did not show up. She was working in a nearby Dayton restaurant that day and was unable to retrieve the money herself. She asked her mother, Anne Delaney, to go for her to retrieve the money. Delaney could not drive, so she asked Payne to drive her to the postal telegraph office that day. Parker watched as Payne pulled up and got out with Delaney. Together, they walked into the office to get the money.

Enraged, Parker rushed to the building, locking eyes with his son in the backseat of the car as he passed it.

Once inside, he located Payne, looked him in the eye and said, "Now I've got you. This is the last time you'll break up a home."

Before anyone knew what was happening, a shot rang out. As other customers in the postal office ran outside to safety, Parker turned to his mother-in-law and said, "I told you I'd do it."

Parker then turned and walked toward the exit, stopped, turned around and walked back to where Payne lay on the floor and fired a few more rounds. After, Parker did not attempt to flee the scene. Instead, he remained there and waited for the Dayton Police to arrive. When they did, he handed over his pistol and let them arrest him. Payne was pronounced dead at the scene; the coroner's ruling was "homicide, multiple revolver rounds of the head. Compound skull fractures (multiple)." Payne's body was sent to his mother in Livingston, Kentucky. Services were conducted in her home.

The trial and news coverage were sensational. Although it was an admitted fact that Parker shot Payne, many debated whether or not he was guilty, citing the "unwritten law," which forbids the breaking up of a home by a third party. Not only was this man spending time with Parker's family while he was at work, but he was wearing his clothes as well. This unwritten law was also referenced during the trial as a form of defense.

The coroner's finding included testimony from seven witnesses, four of whom claimed they witnessed the shooting themselves. Included in the testimony for the coroner's inquest were:

William Adams, a customer of the postal office, was standing outside when the shooting occurred. Adams looked in the window and witnessed Parker standing over Payne's body. Adams left the scene and brought a police officer back with him.

Naomi Stead, cashier, was assisting another customer when Payne was shot. She heard Parker tell Payne he wouldn't break up another home.

Iris Turney, cashier, witnessed the shooting.

Annie Delaney, Parker's mother-in-law, was accompanying Payne to the postal office.

Louis Parker Jr., aka Sunshine, son of Louis and Lalor Parker. Sunshine stayed in the car and witnessed his father walking into the building just before the shooting.

J.T. Ganger, City of Dayton police officer, responded to the scene. Parker told Ganger he made a thousand-mile trip to get Payne.

Tom Wollenhaupt, City of Dayton police officer, also responded to the scene. Parker told Wollenhaupt that he quit his job with the Savannah Police with the intention of getting in contact with Payne and taking care of him. Parker told the officer that he sent the telegraph to Lalor with the intention of meeting with her at the office and reconciling their relationship in person.

The defense strategy was bold. Yes, Parker shot Payne, but he wasn't guilty of murder. To prove that Parker was not guilty for his actions, defense attorneys Jack Egan and Albert Scharrer prepared eleven witnesses who were all ready to testify on behalf of Parker's character. It was an impressive list of A-names of the justice system in Savannah, Georgia.

Those listed were:

1. Honorable Thomas Gamble, mayor, City of Savannah, Georgia
2. H. Mercer Jordon, recorder, City of Savannah, Georgia
3. Honorable Alex R. MacDonnell, chief justice of municipal court, Savannah Georgia
4. Edward Dutton, secretary to the Honorable Rourke, judge of the superior court, Savannah, Georgia
5. Judge James Hoolihan, county commissioner, Savannah, Georgia
6. Robert F. Downing, city marshal, Savannah, Georgia
7. Honorable Emanuel Lewis, judge of municipal court, Savannah, Georgia
8. Robert F. Downing, city marshal, Savannah, Georgia
9. Honorable Emanuel Lewis, judge of municipal court, Savannah, Georgia
10. Honorable B.B. Heery, judge of municipal court, Savannah, Georgia
11. J.J. Clancy, captain, police department, Savannah, Georgia
12. Kathlene Moore, sergeant, police department, Savannah Georgia
13. Dr. G.H. Johnson, coroner, Savannah, Georgia

In addition to the eleven character witnesses, there were eleven more people who were willing to testify via depositions that Parker was pushed to act.

- Dr. J.O. Baker: Physician to the Parker family since 1926. Dr. Baker testified that on July 15, 1924, Mrs. Lalor Parker was examined and found to have a venereal disease. Mr. Louis Parker was also examined and he was found to have no venereal disease.
- Mrs. J.M. Reed: Witnessed meetings between Lalor and Chester. Accompanied Lalor to Dr. Baker's office when she was sick with venereal disease.
- Mrs. J.T. Crosby: Sister of defendant. Crosby visited her sister-in-law Lalor while she was sick in bed and witnessed Chester Payne at her bedside, and he was still there after she left. She told her brother what she saw and confirmed his mental state. She also knew of the venereal disease Lalor had in July 1934. She knew of letters received by Lalor from Chester. She also attested that her sister-in-law ran away to Cincinnati and lived with Payne and then returned home once before. When she left the second time, Parker wanted to bring her home again.
- Mrs. John Dominick: Lifelong friend to defendant. She testified to the attitude and morals of the defendant and his mental state before he left for Dayton. He wanted to bring his wife and children home, as they had never been away from home or from him at Christmas. Parker intended to bring his family home within three or four days. He was nervous and excitable.
- William Miller: Miller knew of secret meetings, automobile rides, parties and trips between Lalor and Chester and testified to dates and times.
- Mrs. Elizabeth Williams: Testified regarding letters Payne wrote to Lalor and that some of those letters were threatening toward Louis Parker.
- Harry Adler: Knew of Chester Payne sneaking over to the Parker home in Louis Parker's absence.
- Mrs. Orrie Lee Alexander: Testified that Parker was very worried when Lalor left for Cincinnati with Payne. Mrs. Alexander visited Lalor when she was sick and knew about the letters she was receiving from Payne.

- Skeet Wilson: Motorcycle policeman, Savannah, Georgia. Mr. Wilson testified that Parker was very worried and upset.
- Billy Kilroy: Commander of foreign wars. Kilroy served in World War I with Parker. Kilroy testified that Parker was gassed. Parker was very excitable and agitated, and Kilroy tried to talk him out of quitting his job. Parker was very nervous and threatened to commit suicide.
- Dr. Rabhan: City physician. Dr. Rabhan personally knew about Parker's condition after the war, that he was gassed and seriously affected by his injury. In times of excitement, Parker was unable to control himself.

In addition to professional contacts, Scharrer called Parker's stepdaughter to the stand. Lucille recounted multiple occasions in which Payne was at the Parker residence while Parker worked. In Parker's absence, there were numerous parties, meals and even outdoor picnics with Payne.

When Lalor took the stand, it was the testimony needed to make Parker a sympathetic character. During questioning, Lalor revealed that she had been married at seventeen to a man named John Pergerson. They stayed together for a few months before she left him for her lover, a man named Lloyd McIntire. Together, McIntire and Lalor lived in common law marriage for seven years, and Lucille was born. Lalor claimed she left McIntire because he was a drunk, so she moved to Savannah to live with her brother, Eddie Williams, who was married to Parker's sister. Shortly after Parker and Lalor met, she moved in with him. She discovered Pergerson had divorced her, and she quickly married Parker. Lalor met Payne at an entertainment show for veterans, where Payne was a crooner. It was from Payne that Lalor contracted her disease. To explain how she got the disease and to justify leaving her husband, she made up a story about a blonde woman named Anna with whom her husband was in love. She told police in Savannah that she found six letters from Anna. The salacious gossip spread like fire through the police force, nearly causing Parker to lose his job. While giving this testimony, Lalor wore a wedding ring bought by Payne from a 10-cent store in Cincinnati.

Before resting, defense attorneys Egan and Scharrer added two more witnesses to their defense. The first witness was Robert Brunson, a student from Purdue University. On the stand, Brunson testified that he was in the lobby at the time of the shooting.

MRS. LALOR PARKER ON WITNESS STAND

Mrs. Parker struggled through her testimony on the witness stand. Dayton Daily News, *courtesy of newspapers.com.*

Another college student, Robert Henry, was also present in the lobby on the day of the shooting. When the court recessed that day at lunch, Henry had been on the stand but not initially permitted to testify. Prosecuting attorneys Nicholas Nolan and Sam Kelly argued against permitting Henry's testimony before Presiding Judge Mason Douglass. Judge Douglass said it was his duty to ensure the jury received all the evidence and ultimately ruled that Henry can testify.

The testimony of both students was intended by defense council to discredit the witnesses who recalled the people in attendance but did not list the two students. During testimony, the prosecution witnesses claimed to name everyone in attendance at the time of the shooting, leaving nobody out. None of the witnesses named either of the young men.

During the trial it was revealed that Payne was staying at a transient camp in Savannah when he met Lalor. Most of their meetings occurred while Parker, a veteran of the First World War, was at work. Many accusations between the attorneys of both sides escalated to a feverish pitch, resulting in the jury being excused while council argued before the judge. The feud resulted in blood tests being drawn from both Louis and Lalor Parker to determine who did and who did not have venereal disease.

The trial was nearly halted when juror Henry Kastner fell ill and proceedings had to be stopped so Dr. William Roehm, jail physician, could have a look at him. Kastner recovered and was able to continue his duties. Clifton Hubbard was ready to report as the alternate juror, had Kastner not been able.

The nine men and three women of the jury were sequestered at the Dayton Biltmore hotel, where each juror had their own quarters. In addition, the jury was supplied with their own recreation room and their own elevator service. They were supplied with out-of-town newspapers and magazines, and any local papers were screened for information before jurors were allowed to read them. They could take one thirty-minute walk together in the morning, under the watchful eye of Bailiff Eli Walker, who was responsible for the male jurors. Anyone who wished to stay behind stayed in the custody of Deputy Clerk Kathryn Farrell, who was in charge of the female jurors. The jury was also not permitted to attend church, as they needed to be secluded from anyone who could give them information from news coverage of the case, so instead they were given a long bus ride on Sunday evening.

The trial ended after fifteen days, and to the surprise of many, Louis E. Parker was acquitted of murder in the first degree. The first ballot returned with a verdict of not guilty, eleven to one, and the second ballot was not guilty, unanimous. Immediately after the jury was released, Harry A. Rietdyk, elected as jury foreman, said the prosecution failed to prove that Louis Parker did not kill Chestnut Payne in self-defense.

James Rahal, Parker's Savannah attorney, released a statement to the press that he would encourage Parker to rejoin the police force in Savannah when he returned home. Parker was quickly awarded custody of his son, Louis Parker Jr, aka Sunshine. Parker, Lalor and McIntire all wanted to take custody of Lucille, but McIntire had been absent from her life and Lalor's past caused her to lose custody to Parker. He took the two children with him to Savannah, and Lalor stayed in Dayton with her mother for a while before moving to Florida to live with her brother, Eddie.

BIBLIOGRAPHY

Chapter 1

Burba, Howard. "The Day They Hung John McAfee." *Dayton Daily News*, November 23, 1930.

Dayton Daily News. "Committed to Memory on her Grandfather's Knee." April 14, 1930.

———. "Over the River on a Rope." April 26, 1902.

Chapter 2

Burba, Howard. "Bloodshed in the 'Bucket Brigade.'" *Dayton Daily News*, April 9, 1933.

"Charles Russell Greene." Genealogy. www.werelate.org/wiki/Person:Charles_Greene_(17).

"Charles Russell Greene (1785–1833)." Find a Grave. https://www.findagrave.com/memorial.6070006/charles-russell-greene.

Chapter 3

Broadstone, Michael A. *History of Green County, Ohio: Its People, Industries and Institutions*. Vol. 1. N.p.: B.F. Bowen, 1918.

Xenia Daily Gazette. "Ransbottom." May 27, 1899.

Xenia Gazette. "First and Last Hanging in County Was in 1850." June 17, 1953.
———, January 31, 1850.
———. "Mother of Xenia Woman Witness This County's Only Legal Hanging." April 9, 1936.
Xenia Torchlight. "By Telegraph for the Xenia Torchlight." October 17, 1849.
———. "The Fairfield Tragedy." June 28, 1849.

Chapter 4

Dayton Daily News. "Shocking Murder in Greene County." February 27, 1858.
Xenia Gazette. "A Life Prisoner." July 17, 1886.
Xenia Torchlight. "A Bellbrook Murder." August 20, 1889.
———. "The Court of Common Pleas." November 3, 1858.
———. "Murder at Bellbrook." February 24, 1858.
———. "Proceedings in Court." June 9, 1858.
———. "Trial of Andrew Kirby for Murder." October 27, 1858.
Bellbrook Moon Scrapbook 1:28.

Chapter 5

Tiffin Tribune, October 1865.
Xenia Sentinel. "Another Letter by Joshua Monroe." November 25, 1864.
———. "Joshua Monroe." November 11, 1864.
Xenia Torchlight. "Murder and Attempted Suicide at Yellow Springs." December 9, 1863.
———. "Trial of Joshua Monroe." November 9, 1864.

Chapter 6

Our County Paper. "After Seventeen Years." March 19, 1884.
Biddeford Daily Journal. "A Murder Confessed." March 18, 1884.
Burba, Howard. "A Death-Bed Murder Confession." *Dayton Daily News,* June 17, 1934.
Crime Magazine. "Deathbed Murder Confessions." www.crimemagazine. com/deathbed-murder-confessions.

New York Times. "Murder of a Young Lady—Escape of the Murderer." January 14, 1867.

Chapter 7

Burba, Howard. "Who Was Vallandigham?" August 12, 1928.
"The Indignation over Tom McGehean." *True Crime Historian,* truecrimehistorian.com/the-indignation-over-tom-McGehean.
Kuroski, John. "The Bizarre, Accidental Death of Clement Vallandigham." *All That's Interesting,* February1, 2018. allthatsinteresting.com/clement-Vallandigham.
McGehean, Thomas. *A History of the Life and Trials of Thomas McGehean, Who Was Charged with the Shooting and Killing of Thomas S. Myers, in the City of Hamilton, Butler County, Ohio, on the Evening of the 24ᵗʰ of December, 1870: Biographical Sketch of Hon. C. L. Vallandigham.* N.p., 1874.
New York Times. "The Arrest of Vallandigham." May 7, 1863.
———. "Clement L. Vallandigham Accidentally Shoots Himself—The Wound Dangerous, but Not Mortal." June 17, 1871.
———. "The Death of Mrs. Vallandigham." August 16, 1871.
———. "Vallandigham." July 26, 1863.
———. "Vallandigham Dead." June 19, 1871.
Underwood, Richard H. "Not So Great Moments in Trial Advocacy: Clement Vallandigham." *Widener Law Journal* 13 (2003): 185–208.

Chapter 8

Broadstone, Michael A. *History of Greene County Ohio: It's People, Industries, and Institution.* N.p: B.F. Bowen, 1918.
Dillis, R.S. *History of Greene County, Together with Historic Notes on the Northwest, and the State of Ohio.* Dayton, OH: Odell & Mayer, 1881.
Xenia Gazette, December 24, 1872.
———."The Demon Cup." September 10, 1872.
———."The Trial of Davidson—He Is Found Guilty of Murder in the Second Degree—Penitentiary for Life." December 31, 1872.

Chapter 9

Xenia Gazette, April 15, 1873.

———, April 22, 1873.

———."Charge of Judge Smith to the Jury in the Ritchison-Fogwell Murder Case." April 1, 1873.

———. "The Death Sentence of W.B. Ritchison." July 1, 1873.

———."Decision of Judge Smith." May 13, 1873.

———, June 24, 1873.

———, November 5, 1872.

———, November 12, 1872.

———."Ritchison Hangs Himself!" September 2, 1873.

———."Ritchison, the Murderer, Attempts to Escape." August 19, 1873.

———, September 16, 1873.

———. "Supreme Court vs. Judge Smith in the Ritchison Case." June 3, 1873.

———. "The Trial of Ritchison." March 25, 1873.

Xenia Torchlight. "Atrocious Murder." November 13, 1872.

Chapter 10

Burba, Howard. "A Dayton Crime of the Mule-Car Age." *Dayton Daily News*, July 7, 1929.

History of the Police Department, Dayton Ohio: From Earliest Times to October First 1907. Dayton, OH: John C. Whitaker, 1907.

Cincinnati Enquirer. "The End." February 1, 1881.

———. "The Francis Trial." December 11, 1880.

———. "The Francis Trial." January 15, 1881.

———. "The Francis Trial." January 16, 1881.

———. "Francis' Trial." January 18, 1881.

———. "Francis' Trial." January 19, 1881.

———. "Inside Facts." October 16, 1886.

———. "Preliminary Examination of John Francis." January 20, 1880.

———. "Unrevealed." August 5, 1888.

Daily Gazette. "John Francis Dead." January 4, 1899.

Dayton Evening Herald. "Police Court." October 21, 1896.

Dayton Herald. "Opposing a Pardon." December 13, 1883.

Chapter 11

Burba, Howard. "Did Mary Knight Murder Her Mother?" *Dayton Daily News*, November 22, 1931.

The State of Ohio v. Mary Knight, U.S. 2979 (1895).

Young, Roz. "Court Gets Murder Conviction Despite Lack of Evidence, Motive." *Dayton Daily News*, May 15, 1993.

————. "Matriarch Murder—Ne'er-Do-Well Daughter Prime Suspect in Mother's Death." *Dayton Daily News*, May 8, 1993.

Chapter 12

"Board Is Considering the Claim of Joseph Hendrick to the $1000 Reward Offered for Stimmel." *Dayton Daily News*, October 26, 1904.

Burba, Howard. "The Colorful Career of Dayton Slim." *Dayton Daily News*, April 30, 1933.

Cincinnati Enquirer. "The Claims for the Stimmel Reward Will Be Settled." September 2, 1903.

————. "Laid to Rest." July 26, 1904.

————. "Stimmel Denies Being in Dayton, but Detectives Will Bring Him Back." August 28, 1903.

Dayton Daily News. "Bitter Wrangling of Lawyers Characterizes Stimmel Trial." December 12, 1903.

————. "Death in Electric Chair the Doom That Now Awaits Charles Stimmel." December 25, 1903.

————. "The Fate of Charles Stimmel May Be Decided Christmas Eve." December 24, 1903.

————. "The Foul Murder of Joseph Shide May Yet Be Avenged by the Law." December 17, 1903.

————. "Found Guilty of Contempt." October 31, 1903.

————. "Gloomy Prospect for the Jurors in the Stimmel Murder Trial." December 19, 1903.

————. "Hendrick Presents What Seems to Be the Most Substantial Claim for the Reward Offered for Charles Stimmel." October 25, 1903.

————. "His Life Hangs on a Mustache." July 18, 1904.

————. "His Old Mother Wept for Joy." April 14, 1904.

————. "Last Ceremony Held Over a Misspent Life." July 25, 1904.

————. "The Life of Stimmel Has Been Prolonged." June 15, 1904.

———. "More Witnesses Implicate Brush in the Murder of Joseph Shide." December 22, 1903.

———. "Recital of the Shocking Murder Produced No Effect on Stimmel." December 11, 1903.

———. "Slowly Weaving a Web of Circumstantial Evidence." December 17, 1903.

———. "Stimmel Has Fighting Chance." July 16, 1904.

———. "To Throw Suspicion upon Another Is the Apparent Aim of the Defense." December 15, 1903.

———. "A Weird Story Related by a Witness in Stimmel Murder Trial." December 16, 1903.

———. "With Curses on His Lips Charles Stimmel Died." July 22, 1904.

History of the Police Department, Dayton Ohio: From Earliest Times to October First 1907. Dayton, OH: John C. Whitaker, 1907.

Chapter 13

Clinton Mirror. "Strange Story of Dr. Oliver Haugh." December 30, 1905.

Cutwright, Bucky. "The Dr. Jekyll and Mr. Hyde of Mt. Calvary." *Columbus Underground,* November 7, 2019. www.columbusunderground.com/the-dr-jekyll-and-mr-hyde-of-mt-calvary-bc1.

Los Angeles Herald. "Dr. Haugh Pays Death Penalty." April 19, 1907.

McCullough, David G. *The Wright Brothers.* New York: Simon & Schuster, 2016.

Pfeifer, Paul. "Wilbur Wright and the Hockey Stick." *Highland County Press,* August 1, 2016. highlandcountypress.com/Content/Opinions/Opinion/Article/Wilbur-Wright-and-the-hockey-stick/4/22/34122.

The State of Ohio v. Oliver Crook Haugh, U.S. 11194 (1906).

"The Strange Case of Dr. Haugh and Mr. Wright." *Jefferson St. Clair* (blog), October 8, 2015. jeffersonstclair.wordpress.com/2015/10/08/the-strange-case-of-dr-haugh-and-mr-wright/.

Chapter 14

"Arguments Open in Justice Trial." October 1910.

Johnson, Alan. "344th Execution Since 1885 Picks up Where Ohio Left Off." *Columbus Dispatch,* February 19, 1999. www.dispatch.com.

Xenia Daily Gazette. "Accused Murderers Had Nothing to Say." September 1910.

———. "Charles Justice Is Refused New Trial." May 30, 1911.

———. "Charles Justice on Trial for Life." October 1910.

———. "Coroner Will Hold Inquest Wednesday." September 1910.

———. "Court Assigns Dugger's Trial." September 1910.

———. "Eleventh Hour Reprieve Granted." April 28, 1911.

———. "First Degree Murder Grand Jury's Verdict." September 1910.

———. "Guilty of Murder in First Degree." November 4, 1910.

———. "Jury Selected to Try Chas. Justice." October 1910.

———. "Justice and Dugger Back in Xenia Jail." September 1910.

———. "Justice and Dugger Enter Their Pleas." September 1910.

———. "Justice Pays Extreme Penalty for His Crime." October 27, 1911.

———. "Justice to Die in Chair on March 31." November 9, 1910.

———. "Large Concourse Attends Funeral." September 22, 1910.

———. "Obituary." September 20, 1910.

———. "Special Grand Jury Is Now in Session." September 1910.

———. "Twenty Witnesses Before Coroner." September 21, 1910.

———. "Venire Drawn for Dugger Jury." October 1910.

———. "Victim of Chicken Thief Passes Away." September 19, 1910.

———. "William Shoup Is Still Improving." September 1910.

Chapter 15

Cincinnati Enquirer. "Former Officer in Jail." December 26, 1934.

———. "Georgian Slain by Former Policeman." December 25, 1934.

———. "Not Guilty Plea Made." December 27, 1934.

———. "Parker Trial." April 7, 1935.

———. "Scharrer Is Named." March 3, 1935.

Dayton Daily News. "Activities of Jurors Are Limited over Week-End." 1935.

———. "Counsel Begins Arguments on Murder Trial." January 1935.

———. "Defense Rests in Hearing of Louis Parker." 1935.

———. "Louis Parker Murder Trial Opens Monday." April 24, 1935.

———. "Victim Broke Up His Home, Killer States." December 1934.

Dayton Herald. "State Rests in Trial of Louis Parker." April 3, 1935.

———. "Two Children in Custody of Louis Parker." April 12, 1935.

———. "Woman Unable to Continue on Witness Stand." April 5, 1935.

Death Certificate, Chestnut Payne, File Number 75053. Division of Vital Statistics, Dayton, Ohio.

Evening Independent "Wore 10-Cent Wedding Ring." April 5, 1935.

Greer, David C. *Sluff of History's Boot Soles*. N.p: AuthorHouse, 2005.

State of Ohio, Montgomery County (1934). Coroner's Finding.

State of Ohio v. Louis E Parker, U.S. 12853 (1935).

ABOUT THE AUTHOR

Sara Kaushal was born and raised in a suburb of Dayton, Ohio, and now lives in another one with her husband, Ravindu and their son, Yuvi. She owns a collection of books she swears she will read one day and is the primary author of the blog *Dayton Unknown*. Sara loves hiking, spicy food and finding four-leaf clovers. She hates cheese on her pizza and spends way too much of her free time focused on murders and true crime stories.

www.ingramcontent.com/pod-product-compliance
Lightning Source LLC
Chambersburg PA
CBHW070335100426
42812CB00005B/1337